Jesus in
Blue Jeans

Other books by Laurie Beth Jones

Jesus, CEO: Using Ancient Wisdom
for Visionary Leadership

The Path: Creating Your Mission Statement
for Work and for Life

Jesus in
Blue Jeans

A Practical Guide
to Everyday Spirituality

Laurie Beth Jones

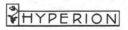

New York

Library of Congress Cataloging-in-Publication Data

Jones, Laurie Beth.
Jesus in blue jeans : a practical guide to everyday spirituality /
Laurie Beth Jones.—1st ed.
p. cm.
Includes index.
ISBN 0-7868-6226-2
1. Jesus Christ—Example. 2. Christian life. I. Title.
BT304.2.J66 1997
232.9´04—dc21   97–3907
CIP

FIRST EDITION
10 9 8 7 6 5 4 3 2 1

Book design by Jennifer Ann Daddio

This book is dedicated
to my grandmother Frances Jones Saunders,
who taught me about poise,
and
to my grandfather Joseph Saunders,
who taught me about
perspective.
My mother Irene Jones
urged me
to seek a life filled with
passion,
and my father
Robert Jones
taught me that I was worthy
of power.
And
I want to especially remember
my grandmother Irene Potters,
who made sure that I had
a constant supply
of blue jeans
while growing up.

Contents

Prologue

Many years ago I dreamed that I was standing in a meadow. Suddenly I saw a man approaching me. As he got nearer I gasped to realize that it was Jesus in Blue Jeans. When he saw the expression on my face he said, "Why are you surprised? I came to them wearing robes because they wore robes. I come to you in blue jeans because you wear blue jeans."

I fell in love with him at that moment. There is something so familiar—and so powerful—about a man in jeans.

Introduction

Jesus in Blue Jeans completes the trilogy which was begun with *Jesus, CEO: Using Ancient Wisdom for Visionary Leadership* in 1995, and continued with the second book, *The Path: Creating Your Mission Statement for Work and for Life*, in 1996. The title of this third book reflects my personal journey as well, going from a full-time, "workaholic" businesswoman intent on profits and high productivity, to someone forced to take a time-out and evaluate her Path, to a person who is perhaps happiest in her blue jeans on her ranch in Texas.

In some ways this book also reflects the evolution of a generation. Those who were taught in the 1980s to acquire as much as possible with OPM (Other People's Money) were suddenly forced in the early 1990s to take a time-out, as the houses of cards we created with OPM collapsed into DYAM (Debts: Yours and Mine). As the new millennium hurtles toward us, many of us have either been forced through downsizing (or have given ourselves permission through "rightsizing") to spend more time in our blue jeans and less time in the office. One of the great gifts of technology has been the flexibility to choose *where* we want to be while we conduct our businesses, interact with our families and communities, and utilize our gifts. We just need to know more about *who* we want to be while we are doing this, and that is a question technology can never answer. For this endeavor, I turn once again to Jesus, a person who knew how to combine the heavenly with the earthly, and maintain his balance.

In *Jesus, CEO,* I reminded leaders that if they treated their staff, followers, and associates the way that Jesus treated his, productivity and morale would soar. In *The Path* I presented a series of simple yet in-depth exercises that would help lead readers to their divinely inspired mission statement. Both books became national bestsellers, and spurred individual and corporate study groups worldwide.

Since traveling the country teaching principles from both books, people have come forward and asked, "Could you write a book that would just help me with my everyday life? What more could you write about Jesus that will help me just get through the day?"

As I pondered strengths in Jesus that helped him live so triumphantly, I found that there were four qualities that we, too, can emulate: Poise, Perspective, Passion, and Power.

In each titled section I present chapters detailing how he lived out these qualities. At the end of each chapter I have a prayer called Power Connections, because to me that is what prayer really is—a powerful connection with the Source of our being.

Trying to divide Christ's teachings into sections is like trying to put your arms around the sunlight. To the heart that needs no lines or boundaries, these section headings will merge into one. (To Rick, my editor, however, this arrangement looks like a highly organized package.) The most important thing for readers to recognize is that Jesus had an everyday life, just like you and I, and we, too, can learn the principles that guided his steps.

When I remember my first encounter with Jesus, it seemed that his eyes were like diamonds held up to the sun—casting light in a thousand directions. I pray that the words in this book will somehow do the same.

Poise

In your patience possess ye your souls.
Luke 21:19 (King James Version)

poise: (poiz), n., v.,—n. 1. a state of balance or equilibrium, as from equality or equal distribution of weight. 2. a dignified, self-confident manner or bearing; composure; self-possession 3. steadiness, stability. 4. the way of being poised, held, or carried 5. the state or position of hovering— v.t. 6. to adjust, hold, or carry in equilibrium; balance evenly

—*Random House Webster's College Dictionary*

Poise is a red-winged blackbird balancing ever so lightly on a reed by the river. The bird rests on this perch effortlessly, ready to take flight at a moment's notice, scanning the sky for its next destination—ever mindful of its wings.

By contrast many of us seem to picture ourselves hanging on to a frail branch extending over a dark canyon, our fingernails deeply embedded in the bark as we glance fearfully down at the rocks below—almost certain we will fall to our doom unless someone or something comes to rescue us.

"I've only got one nerve left, and you're standing on it!" seems to be the motto of our generation. A truck cuts us off in a lane of traffic and we let loose a string of obscenities, and the next thing we hear is a bullet crashing through our window and we turn to find that the child in the car seat behind us is dead. True story. We lose our balance in a retail store—or in a relationship at home or work—and the next thing you know fists or lawsuits or bullets are flying, each side determined to prove the other wrong.

In this country lawyers outnumber counselors ten to one. Prisons are going up faster than day-care centers. Divorce courts require metal detectors before former lovers can even face each other. Churches in the South are being burned to the ground and too many churches all over the world are burning people to the bone with their harsh, divisive words. All because we have lost our poise, and our sense of balance—the balance Jesus came to teach us. He came to teach us how to stand tall, and bend our knees, and when to do both. He came to teach us how to bear insults without returning them in kind. He came to teach us how to live with one another and ourselves.

Jesus came to teach us poise—to make us ever mindful of our wings and God's clear open sky.

He Groomed Himself Properly

One day when I was ten years old, I came home from school to discover that Harriet, my pet duck, had drowned. Not only had she drowned, but she had done so in the backyard pond I had so lovingly prepared for her. My parents were as saddened and baffled by her death as I, so they summoned our vet to the scene. "Was it a homicide or a suicide?" we asked, looking at the victim. "Neither," he replied, lifting up her small waterlogged body. "This duck did not groom herself properly. You see, ducks have to coat themselves with a special waterproofing oil that is produced beneath their wings. For some reason, she didn't, so when she started swimming, her feathers took on water, and she sank like a stone."

Just as ducks depend upon a unique oil that allows them to be "in" yet not "of" the water, we, too, need to cover ourselves with a grooming oil in order to be "in" yet not "of" the world. We need to daily cover ourselves with prayer, praise, and poised reminders of who we are both to—and in—God.

Jesus groomed himself properly. I think he did so by immersing himself in scriptures—especially those that speak of God's love and high holy calling. "My soul rejoices in my God. For he has clothed me with the garments of salvation and arrayed me in a robe of righteousness."—Isaiah 61:10

Paul admonished us to "put on the whole armor of God." We need to cover ourselves with a protective coating that will serve us as we venture out into the a world that is filled with negative forces. Many of us who wouldn't dream of going to the beach without sunblock will go days, weeks, and months without prayer.

Author Diane Loomans has a wonderful opening exercise in her book *Full Esteem Ahead*, which she co-wrote with her daughter Julia. While brushing her daughter's hair one hundred strokes, she whispers to her with each stroke how wonderful and original and unique and humorous and powerful and creative she is. Although oftentimes the girl will drift asleep during the process, it is clear from looking at her face that she has heard every word. By grooming her daughter properly with absolute love, Diane has seen to it that the girl is not likely to drown in a pool of depression or self-doubt when she hits a negative world.

When I was about to embark on my first book tour promoting *Jesus, CEO*, I asked a number of people to pray for me. The day before I left dear friends of mine brought over some holy water from Jerusalem. They anointed my forehead with it, saying, "May you think the thoughts of God." They then anointed my lips and said, "May you speak the words of God." They made the sign of the cross over my heart and prayed, "May you feel the love of God." When I opened my eyes I felt "groomed." Their prayers and blessings had covered me with oil.

The following is one of my favorite passages of "grooming oil":

Yahweh created me when his purpose first unfolded,
before the oldest of his works.
From everlasting I was firmly set,
from the beginning, before earth came into being.
The deep was not, when I was born,
there were no springs to gush with water.
Before the mountains were settled,
before the hills, I came to birth;
before he made the earth, the countryside,
or the first grains of the world's dust.
When he fixed the heavens firm, I was there.
When he drew a ring on the surface of the deep,
when he thickened the clouds above,
when he fixed fast the springs of the deep,

when he assigned the sea its boundaries,
when he laid down the foundations of the earth,
I was by his side, a master craftsman,
delighting him day after day,
ever at play in his presence,
at play everywhere in his world,
delighting to be with the sons of men.
—PROVERBS 8:22–31
THE NEW JERUSALEM BIBLE

By repeating this and other scriptures to himself, Jesus was covering himself with the holy anointing oil of God's strength and love.

He groomed himself properly.

Question

What protective coating do you apply to your mind, your heart, your soul, every day?

Question

What scriptures are your anointing oil?

Question

Who else are you "water-proofing" with words? Which words are you using?

Question

What other scriptures might Jesus have used to groom himself?

Power Connection:

Dear Lord, guide me with the renewal of my heart and mind in You. Help me remember to take Your words of love and power and protection and blessing, and groom my mind and heart with them, so that I may think the thoughts of Christ, feel the love of Christ, and speak the words of Christ, in my every action. Help me cover myself with the oil of Your love so that I, too, can be "at play everywhere in your world, delighting to be with the children of God." Remind me to draw from under my wings that oil of Your love which will keep me afloat in this world, and in the world to come.

Amen.

I, _____, groom myself properly.

He Did Not Whine—He Hummed

During a trip to speak at a convention in Hawaii, I found myself a passenger in a car with Alan and Honey Becker, my friends and sponsors for the event. On this particular day the traffic was unbearable. Workers were rebuilding a section of the highway, and cars were moving only three feet every ten minutes. It was also very hot, and you could see that tempers were beginning to flare in the drivers who were caught, like us, in the traffic jam. I felt my head begin to pound and began thinking of getting out of the car to walk up ahead and "exhort" the slow highway workers. We turned off the air conditioner and rolled down the windows to keep the car from overheating. Suddenly I noticed that Alan had begun to hum. He was humming while I was fuming. When I asked him what he was doing, he explained, "I was trying to see if the engine in that truck beside us is idling in the key of C or the key of D." Surprised by this unusual approach to unbearable traffic sounds, soon each of us in the car was humming—trying to match the traffic noise. It actually became fun!

I believe that Jesus hummed and did so often—as, for example, when he walked through the fields of lilies. I believe Jesus may also have even been humming on his way to visit Lazarus' tomb, even though the waiting women were frantic at his tardiness. He was humming because he knew what he was going to do, and he had serene confidence in the face of the difficult task that awaited him. "Father, I thank you for hearing my prayer, just like you always do."—John 11:41. Because Jesus knew who he was, he could hum. He may have been humming before he turned the water into wine, or as he broke the loaves of bread that fed the five thousand, or even as he faced a furious Pontius Pilate.

In Herbert Benson's book, *The Relaxation Response*, the Harvard-trained physician documents that the act of focusing the mind on a single sound or image brings about a physiological change that is the opposite of the fight-or-flight response. Studies show that heart rate, respiration, and brain waves actually slow down, muscles relax, and stress-related hormones diminish.

Athletes are trained to hum prior to and during events so that they will not leave room for negative thoughts or fear. Joan of Arc is said to have hummed in prison, and it drove her captors crazy. Who of us can ever forget the news reports of little Jessica, trapped in a deep well in Texas, humming to herself while her parents wept and the rescue team struggled furiously to free her? Humming made her desperate situation more tolerable and brought her comfort.

Humming is also a sign of creativity. Recently a producer overheard one of the workers at a major studio in New York humming. Low on funds, and time, he asked if she wrote music. When she said she did, he hired her to come up with his movie's theme song. Her humming led to a career burst of new possibilities.

Some synonyms for "hum" in *Rodale's Synonym Finder* are throb, buzz, purr, zoom, sing, croon, whisper, move, stir, bustle, move briskly, scintillate, vibrate, pulse, pulsate, quiver.

Don't you think we need more of that kind of energy in the world? Bees hum while they work, and few insects in the animal kingdom produce such sweet results. Some of the fastest birds in the world are, after all, *humming*birds.

I propose that we encourage more humming in our homes, classes, religious institutions, and the workplace. Humming gets us into a mental zone of both creating and receiving ideas. I personally find that I cannot write unless I first begin to hum.

When we find ourselves in difficult situations, perhaps we shouldn't whine, but hum, like Jesus did.

"The water I give becomes a perpetual spring within you, welling up into eternal life."—John 4:14

Jesus hummed.

Question

How often do you hum?

Question

How can humming help your blood pressure?

Question

Why and when could humming be an effective strategy
- for success?
- for stress reduction?
- for driving your tormentors crazy?

Power Connection:

Dear Lord, help me match my tone to Your confidence in a situation. Help me first hear Your tone, and then hum along wherever I am.

Amen.

I,_____, hum.

He Sought Common Ground

In coming to earth Jesus was seeking common ground with us. By walking in handmade leather sandals and scraping his knuckles while lining up a plank in his father's carpentry shop and feeling the slight tingle of wine at the wedding feasts, he was seeking common ground with us. Had he appeared draped in armor and displaying a halo the size of the rings of Saturn, he would, perhaps, have impressed more people. But then their conversion would have been based on awe and fear, rather than on the relationship he wanted, which was love. He did not come to earth hurling thunderbolts (though his disciples urged him to do so). He did not point out the numerous flaws, sins, and inadequacies of those around him (though they were obvious to many). He sought common ground with people so that he could reach them, and teach them, and love them, *where* they were. He even learned their language in a desire to communicate clearly and effectively. He used the words they used. He sang the songs they sang. He dressed like they dressed. He wore blue jeans.

In the Simon Wiesenthal Museum in Los Angeles there is a display in which visitors are asked to identify three ways that certain human figures sketched on a board are different. This exercise is easy: Race and sex automatically answer two of the three. Then viewers are asked to identify sixteen things these figures have in common. This exercise takes more time, and most people quickly tire of it and walk away. It does not take a genius to see what makes individuals different, but it does require wisdom and patience to determine what different people have in common.

Even the apostle Paul, a man probably not known for his natural charm, stated that he endeavored to find common ground with an audience before preaching to them. In Philippians 2:1, he exhorts his listeners to "remember the Spirit that we have in common. Be united to your convictions and united in your love, with a common purpose and a common mind." In John 17:11, Jesus himself prays over and over again "that the people may be one, like you and I are one." He also clearly said that the way others would recognize that we were his disciples would be by the love we have for one another, not by the relative merits of our strengths versus their weaknesses. "He who looks down on his neighbor sins," advises

Proverbs 14:21. When any person or group looks down on others, casting moral judgments, they are making themselves "wrong."

Diplomatic negotiations proceed much faster when every participant has an understanding of the common needs, values, and ideas of the other parties involved. "Judge your fellow guests' needs by your own. Be thoughtful in every way." —Ecclesiasticus 31:15 (New Jerusalem Bible). Jesus in blue jeans would not be looking for obvious differences among people but would search for the common ground—in conversation, in thought, in interests, in goals, and in values. *Guideposts* magazine recently shared an article about a middle-class woman who, by reason of bankruptcy, found herself suddenly living in a ghetto neighborhood. Frightened at first, she soon wondered how God could use her to make a connection with people whose everyday lives were plagued by drug and alcohol abuse, domestic violence, and drive-by shootings. She began by inviting the local women (some of them admitted prostitutes) for coffee every morning. Wary at first, one by one they began to gather. She found that what all these women had in common was an intense desire for a better life for their children. It was on this foundation that she actually built a church without walls. She sought, and found common ground with them, and several families' lives were changed. This would not have happened without her focusing on what could be shared, rather than why she was scared.

Differences will always make themselves apparent. It is up to us to search for and recognize the silent, pervasive, and important things we have in common. Only then can heart-to-heart communication occur. It is said that former President Jimmy Carter was able to negotiate the bloodless surrender of the dictator in Haiti because he appealed to his sense of honor and love for his country—qualities Carter was able to discover in a man others saw only as egotistical and self-serving. In many verses of the New Testament the apostles exhort the new believers to remember:

> *"In this life one's nationality or race or education is unimportant. Such things mean nothing . . . let love guide your life."*
>
> —COLOSSIANS 3:11,14

> *"Be tactful with those who are not [like you] and be sure you make the best use of your time with them. Talk to them agreeably and with a flavor of wit, and try to fit your answers to the needs of each one . . . [because] . . . In Christ's image there is no room for distinction between Greek or Jew . . . There is only Christ. He is everything and he is in everything. The body is a unit, though it is made up of many parts . . . The eye cannot say to the hand, I do not*

*need you . . . For we are all baptized by one Spirit
into one body, and we were all given the one Spirit to
drink . . ."*
—COLOSSIANS 3:11, 14, GALATIANS 3:28,
1 CORINTHIANS 12:4–26

He sought common ground.

Question

List sixteen things you and your current adversary have
in common.

Question

How could you use that as a foundation for peacemaking?

Question

Pick a person or a group you are afraid of. Write down
all the things you have in common.

Power Connection:

Dear Lord, please help me see what I have in common
with those I consider my adversaries, or those whom I fear.

Help me remember that Your sun shines on us all, that each of us are recipients of Your Grace, and each of us have important places in Your Ultimate Design. Help me see You in them, and help me be You to them.

Amen, and Amen.

I, _____, seek common ground.

He Did Not Take Things Personally

Jesus did not take the insults and accusations of the scribes and the Pharisees personally. He saw their words as emanating from impure hearts, so he didn't agonize over the mud they slung. He knew their bitterness was rooted in their own misery and not caused by him. He concentrated on his mission, despite their insults. His refusal to take their attacks personally extended even unto death. "Father, forgive them; for they know not what they do." (Luke 23:34)

In his poem "The Wood-Pile" Robert Frost describes his experience of walking through a forest. "A small bird flew before me. He was careful / To put a tree between us when he lighted, / . . . He thought that I was after him for a feather— / The white one in his tail; like the one who takes / Everything said as personal to himself." Frost finds the self-centeredness of the bird amusing, as if in the entire forest there is only one thing worth seeing or having—that bird's tail feather. Yet haven't we all encountered people like that, people who seem to think that every comment or action exists for the sole purpose of doing them harm?

A friend of mine had a boss who used to spend hours every day monitoring everyone's phone calls. Newly appointed to his position, he was sure that the team was now out to get him and would use every opportunity to make him look bad. Granted, the team did not care for him much, but the truth was, their phone calls did not concern him at all— or contained only the slightest references to him, as one might wave off a fly at a picnic. I remember once being offended because a man sitting next to me on a plane seemed unresponsive to my jokes. Only when we were exiting did I realize that he was deaf.

Maturity is realizing that we are not the center of the world . . . or the office . . . or the team. Maturity is realizing that not every word spoken or action taken centers around— or is directed toward—us.

Several years ago I attended the final sermon of a minister who was retiring. She was exhausted and wanted to replenish herself with a long-deserved sabbatical. She was a flamboyant woman who often spoke the truth from the pulpit in highly personal and entertaining terms, and her tenure had been attended with much attention from the media and not a small bit of controversy. As I stood in the vestibule after her farewell, I couldn't help but overhear various comments from the people who had been in the congregation. A man who I knew had recently gone bankrupt said, "Yep—it's the system that beat her. She just couldn't take the financial pressure." A woman who was in the throes of a divorce remarked, "I'm sure it's her husband who pushed her to this. You can't carry such a heavy load without support at home." The florist who decorated the halls of the church gushed, "Could you believe that yellow dress? Wasn't she just like an Easter lily up there?" A reporter who was mingling in the crowd commented, "I'm sure there must be some ulterior motive behind her resignation. You know her. Why did she really leave?" It was suddenly apparent to me that this minister's decision was being interpreted by everyone according to his or her personal circumstances. Probably none of us could clearly see her for who she was, because she was in so many ways being used as a mirror by each of us. We were taking her actions personally.

On a recent tour of Europe I was flabbergasted when one of the local guides in Italy began hurling insults at *our* guide, upset by something she had said. In response, she simply smiled, tilted her head, and walked away. When I asked her later why she had ignored his insult, she replied, "Many of the guides hired by that particular agency aren't—shall we say—*refined*. What he said was merely a reflection of him. It had nothing to do with me."

Proverbs 12:16 (*The Living Bible*) tells us "A fool is quick-tempered; a wise person stays cool when insulted."

Insults and accusations are nearly always about the person sending them, rather than about the target. "A man who throws a stone into the air throws it on his own head."
—Ecclesiasticus 27:25 (*New Jerusalem Bible*)

A friend of mine told me that as she advanced toward her dream of getting a Ph.D., certain family members actually tried to stop her, telling her that she was acting "out of her element." "I just kept saying to myself, Nancy, these insults aren't about me, they are about them—and their own fears and feelings of inadequacy."

Jesus did not have the time to pay heed to every insult or track down every rumor. His mission was very important, and he stuck to it, despite the distractions that presented themselves.

> *The Lord Yahweh comes to my help,*
> *so that I am untouched by the insults."*
> —Isaiah 50:5–7 (New Jerusalem Bible)

Jesus did not take things personally.

Question
Do you let insults "wound" you, or let them pass right through?

Question

What insults are being or have been hurled at you?

Question

Could you use others' insults as sources of information about their needs, flaws, and personalities?

Question

Name a time when the restraint of someone's temper saved the day.

Question

Name a time when the loss of someone's temper escalated the situation.

Power Connection:

Dear Lord, help me not to be so quick to assume that everyone is talking about me, or that every insult or oversight is meant to do me harm. Help me not be like Frost's bird in the forest—certain that everyone is interested only in getting the white feather from my tail. Help me realize that I am just a small part of the forest, and that in general, people are hiking through with their own, much larger agendas. Help me feel invincible and invisible when slander or insults are hurled at me. Help me remember not to take things personally.

Amen.

I,_____, do not take things personally.

He Did Not Lean on Reeds

I once read a story about the Old Testament in which one of the prophets chastises a king who has formed a fear-based compromise with the enemy. The prophet warns, "This kind of reed will pierce the hand of anyone who leans on it." That image was so powerful it has long stayed in my mind. Many ills in our society arise because people choose to lean on reeds, even though "reeds will be pulled up before any other grass." —Ecclesiasticus 40:16. At times all of us are tempted with multiple diversions and delusions about who next or what now can offer us comfort or safety or fulfillment or strength. We are surrounded by a Sea of Reeds. In Psalm 106:7 (*New Jerusalem Bible*), David laments, "They defied the Most High at the Sea of Reeds." It is when we are leaning on false prophets or promises that we defy and forsake God, our Source.

Jesus could have built a sizable network of support had he compromised with the Scribes and the Pharisees. They were the recognized religious leaders of the time and thus had a near captive following. Yet Jesus knew that although they appeared to be pillars of strength, they were actually thin as reeds and would pierce anyone who tried to lean on them. He chose to stand firmly on his own relationship with God and not "lean on reeds." "I would rather take refuge in Yahweh, than rely on men; I would rather take refuge in Yahweh, than rely on princes." —Psalm 118:8–9 (New Jerusalem Bible)

We may think, "Here is the job/friend/spouse/lover/career/money/drug/achievement that will make me happy and fulfill all my needs." But they are each only reeds if we look to them to supply all our needs. "Neither to son nor wife, brother nor friend, give power over yourself during your own lifetime . . . As long as you live and there is breath in your body, do not yield power over yourself to anyone." —Ecclesiasticus 33:20–24 (New Jerusalem Bible)

To lean on a reed is to choose to believe a lie.

(I know she/he didn't steal that money. I know she/he isn't cheating on me.)

To lean on a reed is to allow others to define your self-worth.

(What if he/she/they don't like me? Where will I be then?)

To lean on a reed is to confuse anyone else with God.

(I am so terrified of that man/woman/boss/parent.)

"Those who serve worthless idols forfeit the grace that was theirs." —Isaiah 2:9. When you lean on others unnecessarily, you are automatically giving up your own balance and power.

When we allow someone else to define us—based on their relationship with God—we are leaning on reeds. When we draw up agreements based on fear, we are leaning on reeds. "If you do not stand by me, you will not stand at all."—Isaiah 7:9

Jesus did not lean on reeds.

Question

Where are you not standing fully upright?

Question

Who or what are the reeds that you are leaning on?

Power Connection:

Dear Lord, help me not make fear-based alliances that will eventually pierce my soul. Help me to stand firm in You, and not rely on princes. Help me to stand on my own two feet, remembering You are my God, my Source, my Strength, and my Rock.

Amen.

I,_____, do not lean on reeds.

He Did Not Have a Stiff Neck

A friend and I were recently discussing the scripture where Jesus said the only "unforgivable sin" was to sin against the Holy Spirit. As we speculated about what kind of sin that would be, she remarked, "I think it means having a stiff neck." I laughed until she knowingly cited references from the scriptures about God's anger against individuals who were stubborn and rebellious. "The prophets always called them stiff-necked people," she asserted.

It made me think about "stiff-neckedness," and I concluded, among others things, that stiff-necked people wouldn't turn their heads to accept or recognize forgiveness when it was offered to them.

Jesus did not have a stiff neck. He was able and willing to look in any direction. If God said, "Pay attention to this woman about to be legally stoned to death," Jesus turned his head toward the problem. If God said, "Now let's address the issues of hypocrisy in religion," Jesus turned his head toward the scribes and the Pharisees. If any group could be considered stiff-necked, it had to be these men, who felt they knew all the answers. They needed only their own opinions to tell them that they were "right."

These were indeed stiff-necked people, the ones doomed to miss the blessing because they couldn't turn their heads to look up and behold the star. They couldn't turn their heads to see that maybe something good could come from Nazareth —or from anywhere besides their own midst. They couldn't turn their heads to notice the broken hearts and tears all around them, caused by their own lack of compassion and false, ego-inflated sense of holiness. They couldn't turn their heads or bend their knees. They had stiff necks, and as anyone who has ever had a stiff neck knows, it soon affects your whole outlook. "My people refused to listen to me, so I left them to their stubborn, [stiff-necked] selves." —Psalm 81:8–12

There's a beautiful verse in Psalm 32:8–9 that says, "I will instruct you and teach you in the way to go." God's yearning is for people who will be responsive to the Higher Call. "O, Israel, if only you would listen to me!" —Psalm 81:8–12

A man was telling me of his frustration at having worked eighteen hours overtime to cover for two of his colleagues who were ill. A major report had to be turned in, and he willingly took on the task of making sure it was completed. On Monday morning he was summoned by his boss, and as he was walking to the boss's office he thought to himself, *Maybe he's going to thank me for all my hard work this weekend.* Instead he was greeted by a gruff supervisor who said, "McDevitt, you left the lights on. We don't own the electric company, you know. Turn the lights out when you leave." That was all he said. This supervisor had a stiff neck. He couldn't turn his head to try to appreciate or understand this worker's larger contribution. "A stubborn heart will come to a bad end at last." —Ecclesiasticus 3:26

The wind of the spirit blows where it will. We must tilt our heads upward or downward, or even to the ground, to hear what our next set of instructions will be. We must be agile and supple and pliant in order to be used for a Higher Purpose. History is replete with examples of people who led others to their doom because they set their mind on a stiff-necked course of action and refused to change direction even when change was called for.

A group of settlers froze to death because their leader refused to admit a map he had drawn up charting a pass through the mountains was in error. His pride led to the death of an entire colony. "A man who remains stiff-necked after many rebukes will suddenly be destroyed—without remedy."— Proverbs 29:1

"If only you had been alert to *my* voice, your happiness would have been like a river, your integrity like the waves of the sea." —Isaiah 48:18–19

I recently took Antonio, one of my favorite seven-year-olds, to the airport with me. As we approached the metal detector, I went on through. The guard, who was taping a cord on the floor underneath a table, saw Antonio start to walk around the detector and said, while on his knees, "No, son—you'll have to come through this way." Antonio immediately hit the floor and crawled on his knees under the table. We all laughed, and Antonio stood up, baffled by our mirth. Later I reflected on how resilient, responsive, and trusting this child was. Antonio, without questioning, fell to his knees and met the man wherever he was, even if it was under a table. Shouldn't we be like that toward God?

"Not my will, but thine," Jesus prayed.—Matthew 14:36 He did not have a stiff neck.

Question
    What do you have a "stiff neck" about?

Question
    What might you be missing by seeing things only a certain way?

Question
    Who might you be hurting by your refusal to turn your head in another direction?

Power Connection:

Dear Lord, please keep my neck flexible so that my head can turn in the directions You need. Help me to be open to Your word and will, and not stubbornly set my sights on a path or a direction that may be false. I want to be a responsive servant, quick to hear You and quick to obey.

Amen.

I,_____, do not have a stiff neck.

He Mastered the Metaphor

A simile is a figure of speech in which two distinct things are compared using "like" or "as," as in "She is like a rose." (*Webster's New College Dictionary*).

A metaphor is the application of a word or phrase to an object or concept it does not usually denote, as in "A mighty fortress is our God." (*Webster's New College Dictionary*) Jesus was a master communicator because he spoke in metaphors.

In her book *Creativity in Business*, Carol Kinsey Gorman, Ph.D., writes that metaphoric ability is "a mark of genius," and cites Aristotle's contention, "The greatest thing by far, is to be the master of metaphor."

All communicators are really translators—adept at linking the set of thoughts in their own minds to familiar phrases or words that can be recognized or related to by others. As the master of recognizing how one thing resembled something else, Jesus was able to shape ethereal truths into forms we could touch and embrace and understand. He spoke constantly in similes, and was the master of metaphor. How to translate the eternal, forgiving compassion of God? Tell a story about a wayward son. How to teach the colossal importance of faith? Talk about the mustard seed. How to explain your role to people? Describe yourself as a shepherd. What is the kingdom of the heaven like? "It is like a sower who went out to sow . . ."

In *Creativity in Business*, Gorman includes an exercise wherein she presents common objects and asks readers to list twenty ways in which their current situation resembles or is like each of the objects. When I did this exercise with friends, some of our responses were: "My job is like a pin because my only power comes from getting to the point." "Our company is like popcorn because nothing starts to happen until everyone's bottom gets too hot." "My work is like a computer. There's lots of information behind the screen that I don't know how to access." "My relationship is like a glass. Everything I pour into it gets consumed within minutes." "My life is like a paper clip. I have to bend myself in circles just to hang on to what I know."

I wrote, "My work is like a bottle of spray perfume. Someone has to put pressure on my head to get the fragrance out."

In the Academy Award–nominated movie *Il Postino* (*The Postman*), a common postman seeks to woo the lady of his dreams and beseeches Pablo Neruda, a world-famous poet, to help him. Neruda advises him, "Speak in similes, master the metaphor." The postman struggles with the concept, until Neruda asks him to explain how this woman makes him feel. He begins, "Her eyes are the color of this sea before us, changing moods and greens and blues." "That's it!" cries Neruda. "You've done it! You've just created a metaphor!" The postman exultantly writes it down, hands it to the heretofore uninterested lady, and ultimately wins her heart by comparing her to nature . . . using similes and metaphors.

There are few gifts more valuable to a great communicator than being able to link seemingly dissimilar objects, creating fresh ideas and color-filled associations. Writers, poets, artists, sculptors, and musicians are essentially engaged in the business of mastering metaphors, communicating thoughts and ideas that teach us how to look again.

Following are a few examples of how Jesus used similes and metaphors to delight, entertain, educate and communicate truth to others.

The kingdom of heaven is like:

a farmer (Matthew 13:24)

a mustard seed (Matthew 13:31)

yeast (Matthew 13:33)

a hidden treasure (Matthew 13:44)

a merchant (Matthew 13:45)

a net (Matthew 13:47)

a king (Matthew 18:23)

The scribes and Pharisees are like:
blind guides (Matthew 23:26)
whited sepulchres full of dead bones (Matthew 23:27)
a brood of vipers (Matthew 23:33)

When Jesus spoke in similes and metaphors, people "got" what he was saying, even if they chose not to act on it.

Effective communicators use "like" or "as." They see how one thing resembles another, and they communicate that clearly.

Jesus mastered the metaphor.

Question

Why is it important to use similes and metaphors?

Question

Practice injecting at least three similes or metaphors a day into your conversations. "This _____ is like _____," or "This situation resembles _____."

Question

Pick five objects within your immediate sight, and compare them to:
- your job
- your family
- your relationship to God

Power Connection:

Dear Lord, help me see the connections between my ideas and powerful word pictures. Help me translate thoughts into memorable stories and examples others can relate to and remember, just like You did.

Amen.

I,_____, master the metaphor.

He Held Himself in Readiness

Nehemiah had construction workers who also acted as watchmen, laboring with their swords always at their side. "The carriers, too, were armed so that each did his work with one hand while gripping his weapon with the other." —Nehemiah 4:11 They were holding themselves in readiness.

In Matthew 25, Jesus spoke about the ten bridesmaids, five of whom were not ready when the Bridegroom appeared. The five who were ready went with him to the wedding hall, and the door was closed behind them. When the other bridesmaids arrived later, they cried, "Lord, Lord, open the door for us." But he replied, "I do not know you." —Matthew 25:1–13. In the Song of Solomon the woman was not ready to answer the door when her Beloved finally knocked, which led him to disappear for a time. She suffered dearly for this delay, all because she was not prepared.

A readiness exercise often used in tennis requires the players to face the coach while running in place on the balls of their feet, watching for the coach's signal to move to the left or right, up or back. Until the coach waves his or her hand and gives the sign, the athletes are to hold themselves in readiness. As a former tennis player, I can attest to the importance of being on the balls of your feet, rather than sitting back on your heels, when a shot comes flying over the net. The almost visually imperceptible difference of leaning slightly forward rather than standing straight up or leaning back often makes the difference between points won or lost. King David wrote, "I lift my eyes to you . . . like the eyes of a servant girl is fixed on the hand of her mistress." —Psalm 123:1–2. He wanted to be ready for God's instructions.

A man I met in Flint, Michigan, said, "I know you talk a lot in your seminars about self-image. You want to know how I see myself?" he asked. "Of course," I replied. "I see myself as that donkey tied to a tree in Jerusalem, just waiting for the Lord to have need of him." This man had volunteered to drive me back to the airport on a cold and snowy day, and as we were driving his car phone rang. It was the church pastor. "Sure, Rev," he said, "I'll drop some groceries off to her on the way home. An elderly lady in our church can't get out today," he explained. This man also ran the videocamera at my seminar and helped serve as usher for the program as well. I smiled to think that this soul—so willing to be used—

did not have to stand waiting very long. His was a heart in readiness.

When we are admonished in Psalm 46:10 to "Be still, and know that I am God," we are being told to hold ourselves in readiness. King David wrote: "Yahweh, at dawn, I hold myself in readiness for you."—Psalm 5:3. Wisdom is said to meet those who wait for her early at the gate.—Proverbs 1:21. She does not visit those she has to shake out of bed. She will meet and speak to those who are ready and waiting to hear her.

Ten thousand men were willing to fight in Gideon's army, but Gideon was instructed to select only those three hundred soldiers who kept their eyes on the horizon while they drank. In this case, many were called, but few were chosen. God chose not the people who were willing, but the ones who were ready.—Judges 7:5

When Jesus went daily to seek private advice from God, he was holding himself in readiness. When he stayed in Jerusalem for thirty years, he was holding himself in readiness. When he sought God's counsel through prayer and supplication, he was holding himself in readiness. When he said to the soldiers, "I am the one you're looking for," he was holding and presenting himself in readiness. And even as he hung upon the cross, he was holding himself in readiness—in a state of profound anticipation and expectation. "Father, into your hands I commit my spirit." —Luke 23:46

Jesus held himself in readiness.

Question

When, and how, do you hold yourself in readiness for God?

Question

Are you on the balls of your feet, or on your heels, in the game of life?

Question

If you were a commander, how would you want your soldiers to hold themselves in readiness?

Power Connection:

Dear Lord, help me hold myself in readiness for You. Help me stay alert and open—ready to act at a moment's notice to implement Your guidance. Get me out of my chair and on my feet, ready to be a responsive, powerful, positive, ready force for good.

Amen.

I, _____, hold myself in readiness.

He Trusted His Instincts

Jesus knew whom to trust and whom not to trust. When he met Nathaniel he said, "Behold, an Israelite in whom there is no guile." —John 1:47. When he told Peter, "Upon this rock will I build my church," —Matthew 16:18, he was signaling an innate trust in someone who ultimately came through for him. In Nehemiah, a number of opponents tried various means to get him to stop rebuilding the wall. One man sent him a letter, telling him to halt the work immediately and meet him in the Sanctuary. But as Nehemiah explains, "I realized that God had not sent him, so I refused to stop working." —Nehemiah 6:12. In the Old Testament when Abner trusted Joab—a man he knew had ill will against him—he ended up being tricked by Joab and killed. At his funeral King David lamented, "Should Abner have died as a fool dies?"—2 Samuel 3:33. Abner died a fool's death because he had ignored his instinct.

Like these figures in Scripture, we must be wise to the ways and dangers of the world. How many times have you had a gut reaction to a person or a situation and let "logic" (yours or someone else's) overrule you, to your subsequent regret. I once took on a client who made me uneasy. Our company's financial needs caused me to overlook temporarily what my gut was telling me, and though this man came in flashing money he ended up being a source of regret. We lost a lot of sleep (and cash) over that character, and I pledged never again to take on someone who looked good on paper (green or otherwise), if my instinct told me to stay away.

I recently learned that our intestine is lined with the identical tissue that encases our brain, which may explain why our gut also seems to "think and talk" to us. I was fascinated to read in *Time* magazine that Nick Leeson, the young man whose illegal trading practices later brought down Barings, one of the oldest and most respected banks in England, had almost been hired by another bank until their recruiter said, "He looks good on paper, but there's something about him I don't trust." How grateful the shareholders of that bank must be for the recruiter who trusted his instinct.

Scientists are not sure how instinct functions—in either the animal brain, or in ours. Is it a combination of appearances, past history, scent, genetics, magic? Instinct does not follow a rational highway. It just is. Perhaps it is the voice of the Holy Spirit, whispering to us truths we have no other way of knowing, or perhaps it is guardian angels, showing us where to find the jewels and avoid the stones.

In a self-defense course I took, the instructor told the participants, "If you sense danger, it is probably there. Don't discount your feelings."

In order to maintain poise, we must trust our instincts. In order to trust our instincts, we have to have a higher sense of self-esteem. Those people who constantly berate themselves or put themselves down for their feelings are not likely to value, and thus honor, their instincts. Many of the great breakthroughs in science and technology have come from people willing to act on a hunch or a feeling. History has given us great examples of leaders who were able to discern a course of action that saved lives or averted disaster. I believe God easily and often speaks to us through our intuition, ideas, feelings, and emotions. We will hear a voice behind us, saying "This is the Path. Walk ye in it." —Proverbs 16:12

"Jesus [was] inwardly aware of what they were thinking."—Mark 2:8

He trusted his instincts.

Question
    When have you trusted your gut instincts and been glad you did?

Question

Name the times in life that your instincts led you in the right direction.

Question

When have you ignored your instincts, and regretted it?

Power Connection:

Dear Lord, help me listen to what my instinct is telling me to do. Help me understand that You can use our gut, as well as our brain, to guide us.

Amen.

I, _____, trust my instincts.

He Did Not Flinch at the Critical Moment

Martin Scorsese's film *The Last Temptation of Christ* stirred international controversy when it suggested what might have happened if Jesus had decided to forgo the crucifixion and keep to his carpentry shop. The point it raised was a valid one, and one that I think we need to ponder. What would have occurred if Jesus had "flinched at the critical moment"? Being human, he could have easily done so. He could have at any moment recanted his words, both greatly relieving the political system so reluctant to crucify him and foiling the religious powers so adamant on doing so. "I take it back—you all were right. I am just a man from Nazareth caught up in a frenzy of popularity. I think I'll just gather up my mother and friends and we can all go home." He could have quit, stopped the fight, but his heart was resolved, after due reflection. He did not flinch at the critical moment.

There comes a time in each of our lives when we can "flinch at the critical moment," a point at which our very values are called into question. Not long ago I received a call from a businesswoman who was extremely discouraged. It seemed that Bill, a man she had literally raised up in the business and trusted intensely, had left to start his own competing firm, and was now badmouthing her to her clients. In the upcoming weeks she had an opportunity either to go forward with her plans to expand the company or to call it quits. She was so disheartened by Bill's betrayal that she wasn't sure she even wanted to be in the business world anymore. I reminded her that even Jesus had a Judas, and that indeed Judas had somehow been part of God's plan. If she quit the business, Bill and his low-ethics mentality would indeed triumph.

She had reached a critical moment. Was she going to flinch, or stand firm on her principles and her mission? We prayed together, and she resolved to indeed move forward, trusting God to honor her intentions to do good.

Despite all the insults and wounds to her heart, this woman decided not to flinch at the critical moment. She later received a two-million-dollar contract, beating out all competitors, including Bill.

"With constant heart, and confidence in Yahweh, she need never fear bad news. Steadfast in heart, she overcomes her fears. In the end she will triumph over her enemies." — Psalm 112:7–8

Revelations tells us that the prize will be awarded to

those who "endure to the end." —Revelations 2:26. The measure of a soul comes when it is tested. Will it crack—snap—break—at a critical moment?

According to numerous Bible scholars, the book of Job is the oldest scriptural reference we have, predating even the writing of Genesis by many years. I find it interesting that the entire theme of the book is about "not flinching at the critical moment." In this story the Devil told God, "Certainly, Job praises you every day. But look at this life! He has everything!" So God allows innumerable trials to befall Job, who finally utters, "Even though he slay me, yet will I praise him." —Job 1:8; Job 13:15. When tested, Job held firm to his faith and belief in God's ultimate love, despite the circumstances. The critical times were when Job's faith came in, not when it went out.

"My friend, if you aspire to serve the Lord, prepare yourself for an ordeal. Be sincere of heart, be steadfast, and do not be alarmed when disaster comes. Cling to him and do not leave him, so that you may be honored at the end of your days. Whatever happens to you, accept it, and in the uncertainties of your humble state, be patient, since gold is tested in the fire, and chosen people in the furnace." —Ecclesiasticus 2:1–5

A friend and I once hung up a porch swing. I can assure you I leaned on it very hard before I trusted it "not to flinch at the critical moment." God wants people able to be trusted—counted on—leaned on—stood on, if needed. How can workmen create anything of lasting value if the materials they are working with have not been proven to endure?

"A heart resolved after due reflection will not flinch at the critical moment." —Ecclesiasticus 22:19–20 (*New Jerusalem Bible*)

In every situation, Jesus proved he could carry the load. He did not flinch at the critical moment.

Question

What critical moment is facing you now?

Question

What might happen if you flinch?

Question

What might happen if you hold firm?

Question

When in the past have you refused to flinch at the critical moment? What were the results?

Question

Who are others in history who did not flinch at the critical moment?

Power Connection:

Dear Lord, help me to endure, to stand firm, to have a "heart resolved" for You. Help me to realize the importance of holding firm, like a tie beam that keeps an entire structure from collapsing. Help me stand strong in my darkest moments. Thank You for the strength and support You have given me. Thank You for the example of Jesus Christ Your son, and his mother Mary, who received Your word unflinchingly.

Amen.

I, _____, do not flinch at the critical moment.

He Knew They Underestimated Him

Iwonder how Jesus must have felt knowing that people were unaware of who he really was, even his own family members. "He went home again, and once more such a crowd collected that they could not even have a meal. When his relatives heard of this, they set out to take charge of him, convinced he was out of his mind." —Mark 3:20

Judas underestimated Jesus by believing he could be motivated by political power. Herod underestimated him by dismissing him as merely a magician or a lunatic rebel. Pilate underestimated Jesus by thinking that washing his hands after having given in to public opinion could remove the stain. The crowds mocking Jesus as he hung on the cross underestimated him. The guards underestimated Jesus by falling asleep in front of the tomb. (After all, how hard could it be to guard a *dead* man?)

Perhaps only the Roman centurion whose servant Jesus

healed appreciated his power. When Jesus offered to pay a visit to the ill servant, the centurion replied, "No need to. I am a commander, and I know if I merely send word that my soldiers will carry out my orders. Simply say the word, sir, and I know my servant will be healed." Jesus marveled at him, saying, "I have not seen such faith even in Israel." — Matthew 8:5–13. Here was a man who rightly valued Jesus' power.

Jesus said, "It is *the Father in me* who doeth the work." — John 14:10. Through Christ, we are also given the same power. If friends, family, or coworkers think you are too old or too young or too dumb or too anything to do great work, they are underestimating you. Unless you are dealing with people who daily recognize and acknowledge the miracle-working power of God, chances are very good you are being underestimated, and more significantly, chances are you are underestimating yourself.

In Christ, you can do all things. In Christ, your weakness is made perfection. In Christ, your ability to love, to forgive, to heal, to transform is unlimited. That is why you must not fear when you walk through the valleys of the shadow of death. Any enemy lurking in the dark is underestimating you, and your God.

The media escort who accompanied me on the Los Angeles stop of my most recent book tour was a woman about five-feet two inches tall. A petite blonde with movie star charisma, she disclosed during our conversation that after she had been mugged and later carjacked in Los Angeles, she had become a black belt kick boxer. Now, when she and her husband encounter rough situations, her six-foot one-inch husband whispers, "Go ahead, honey, get 'em. I'll hold your purse." She says she actually enjoys the feeling of being underestimated.

I wrote a poem once that read, "That lamb can well afford to be harmless who knows he has a Tiger for a Daddy."

When we have access, through prayer and meditation, to all the gifts and knowledge of God, we can be relatively confident that whoever is challenging us is underestimating us. Our responsibility in difficult situations is to harness the power of God in us, and the power of God everywhere. "I can do all things through Christ who strengthens me." —Philippians 4:13

"The passersby jeered at him; they shook their heads and said, 'Aha! So you would destroy the Temple and rebuild it in three days? Then save yourself; come down from the cross!'"—Mark 15:29–32

Jesus knew they underestimated him.

Question

How are people, particularly critics or adversaries, underestimating you?

Question

How are you underestimating yourself?

Question

What is God's estimate of you?

Power Connection:

Dear Lord, please help me remember who I am in You. Help me see through the apparent circumstances of threat and harm into Your realities of strength, wisdom, and knowledge. Help me recognize one by one the powers I have been given through You, to do good.

Amen.

I, _____, know they underestimate me.

He Knew God Would Provide

For many years I believed that miracles were extraordinary events that happened only rarely as special manifestations of God's presence. The ultimate, "occasional" sign of God's blessing would be a "miraculous" healing. Jesus, of course, was known for his miracles. Many people followed him around, hoping for a miracle sighting. I sometimes feel that those early followers were like those of us who gather to watch fireworks displays—setting up in places where we can get the best view, craning our necks upward, voting with our "oohs" and "aahs" as to the superiority of each burst and shower of light.

I believe that Jesus himself didn't view a miracle as "a miracle" per se, but simply as another manifestation of God's love and provision for human needs. Do you think he ever doubted that he could turn water into wine? Feed the five thousand with a few loaves and fishes? Raise Lazarus? Have the donkey waiting for him just outside Jerusalem? Jesus never doubted because he knew God would provide.

One of the Israelite descriptions of God is *Jehovah-Jireh*, which means "The Lord will provide." Jesus knew it was in God's very nature to provide—it was not an extraordinary, exemplary, and special occasion when He did so. His beneficence was as natural as the sunrise, which helps explain why he so often tried to downplay the miraculous aspect of his deeds. "Okay, I will heal you, but don't tell anyone." Matthew 8:4, Matthew 9:30. "Mother, I don't want to change water into wine, because it is not yet my time."—John 2:4. "Greater things than this shall you do," he said.—John 14:12. The message was, Don't worship the miracles. Understand that GOD PROVIDES.

A friend of mine named Renee is a Lutheran minister in the Bay Area. She had been going through a challenging time with her congregation's needs (as any minister does), and one day in exhaustion she got on her knees and said, "Lord, give me strength. I just need to know that you *see* me." She got up from her prayer and headed out to do the next communion service. Her neighbor across the street, "Mama Leoni," was always encouraging Renee to rest and eat pizza or lasagna with them. This day was no exception, and when she saw Renee going to her car, Mama Leoni rushed over to invite her to dinner. Renee demurred, explaining that she would love to join the family but didn't have time right now, and Mama Leoni began to return to her house. Suddenly, she turned back around and came rushing up to the window of Renee's car. "Renee, Renee," she said, grabbing Renee's face in her hands, "Jesus says *he sees you.*" Renee burst into tears. Just when Renee needed a word of encouragement, God provided one.

The following story is one women can particularly appreciate. One evening I was dashing off to make a presentation, when I realized I had a giant run in my stocking. I looked up at the clock and realized there would be no time to buy a new pair, and that I was thusly going to speak to a group of two hundred business executives. (So much for divine excellence.) Resigned to my fashion faux pas, I ran downstairs to glance through some files in the basement for last minute materials. In between two client files I found a package of panty hose, in exactly the size and the color I needed. Believe me, I have never in my life "filed" panty hose. "Thank you, Lord," I breathed as I changed on the spot, and left to make my presentation in the nick (or run) of time.

This may seem like a trivial incident, but I have many stories like this one, as perhaps, you do—times when out of the blue something appeared for you just when you needed it. "Did we forget to pay the taxes, Collector? No problem. I have the money right here in this fish's mouth, where I always keep it." "Did you forget to buy enough wine, Mrs. Wedding Planner? No problem. Just bring me those jars over there." (Don't you think that Jesus had just a little fun at such times?) "How am I going to get to Jerusalem, Peter? Hertz rent-a-donkey, of course. My father made reservations. You'll find it standing in Lot Three-C." No wonder Jesus used to get so impatient with people who worried about inconsequential things like what they were going to wear or eat. "Consider the lilies!" he would say, and wonder why nobody understood him.—Matthew 17:27, John 2:11, Matthew 21:2, Matthew 6:28

Jesus was such a magnificent manifester because he knew intimately and ultimately this truth: God will provide. I think that when he was a child in heaven he had spent a lot of time in the storeroom. He knew full well what the Inventory was.

Jesus' miracles were not "magic." They were a natural occurrence of a profound and innate truth.

Jesus knew God will provide.

Question

When has God provided something you needed "out of the blue"?

Question

How often do you remember God's former provision for you when you start to feel anxious about the future?

Question

Write down a list of all the things God cannot do.

"Pretend" for a period of just five minutes that God will provide everything you need. Now write down how you would act and feel if you really believed it.

Power Connection:

Dear Lord, You created all that is, and You know exactly where it is stored or filed. Help me realize that miracles are just Your routine way of doing business. Let me function and walk and talk and live as someone who knows You will provide.

Amen.

I, _____, know God will provide.

He Went the Whole Way

"Follow the whole way that God has laid out for you; only then will you live long and prosperous lives." —Deuteronomy 5:33. In the book of Jeremiah the people are also exhorted to "Follow *right to the end* the way that I mark out for you." —Jeremiah 7:23. Evidently, God's people had a reputation for making great starts but not completing the course.

Revelations 2:26 states, "Those that endure *to the end* will be saved." We get no points for having begun something if we do not complete it. Paul said, "I am racing for the *finish* line." —Philippians 3:14

Have you ever had this experience? You start off on a journey to meet someone but soon realize that you are unsure of the directions you received. You go slower and slower as you look for landmarks. Unable to find any you turn around and go back, only to learn later that you had been within half a mile of your destination. You started off fine, but you hadn't gone the whole way.

I had a friend in college who sadly developed a mental disorder that prevented her from completing simple tasks. She would get in her car, start the engine, drive thirty yards, and then back up. Then she would put the car in forward again, go thirty yards, stop, and reverse. There are many causes and treatments for this condition, and thankfully, she got help.

Yet I think many of us have something similar to this malady, even if it's in less clinical or obvious ways. Two friends of mine recently told me that they had begun to notice that I now put the lids back on jars and close cabinet doors. For years, they had observed that I always left a little something in the glass, never drinking the whole thing, and that I always left a door partway open—not wanting to shut or "end" something. My friends call it "the closure thing." Something in me is still too often unwilling to go the whole way . . . to carry a task through to its completion.

Hundreds of books are written on such subjects as "how to get a man to commit"—or "how to close a sale." Many of us have encountered people who are unwilling to make a commitment. Who among us hasn't volunteered for a project only to have our enthusiasm ultimately fizzle out? I am astonished when I see all the unfinished buildings in Mexico—half started, now becoming skeletal ruins because the funding or the desire or the commitment ran out. Too many men father children willingly, yet later have to be tracked down by the federal government or sued in court by their former spouses for child support. Psychiatrists' couches are filled with patients dealing with issues of abandonment. People who have had promises broken by others tend not to be able to keep promises themselves. They find it difficult to go the whole way.

Jesus warned that we should never begin a project without counting the cost. "Can you walk with me the whole way?" he asked Peter and James and John.—Matthew 16:24. He asks the same question of us still.

Jeremiah admonished the people of Israel to "Look at your *footprints* in the Valley, and acknowledge what you have done." —Jeremiah 1:23. They had turned back from serving and worshipping God. They had not gone the whole way.

Yet Scripture also offers us visions of people who can, and did, go the whole way. David wrote in the Psalms of being a proud warrior. "Drinking from the stream as he goes, he can hold his head high in victory." —Psalm 110:7. "Happy the Pilgrims inspired by you with courage to make the Ascents," he also wrote in Psalm 84:5. King David was a man who had a reputation for finishing things (including Goliath). People who acknowledge and dwell in God's power see themselves being able to go the whole way. Jeremiah said, "I have stayed in God's path, following his steps. I have not turned aside." —Jeremiah 23:11

"It is finished," Jesus said.—John 19:30

He went the whole way.

Question

What important project or cause have you left unfinished?

Question

What is keeping you from going the whole way?

Question

List times in your life when you turned back too soon.

Question

List times in your life when you went the whole way. What were the results?

Power Connection:

Dear Lord, give me Your courage to make the ascents. Let me hold my head high in victory, drinking from the stream as I go, knowing that You go with me, and that I will indeed complete that which I have begun.

Amen.

I, _____, go the whole way.

He Knew the Power of Release

Name one miracle the disciples successfully performed in Jesus' *physical* presence. The answer is, not one. Jesus knew what he was talking about when he said, "It is for your benefit that I leave you, for after I leave I will send you the Holy Spirit, who will guide and teach you and empower you."—John 16:6. Rarely do people give their best performance in the presence of their parents. Any day care worker will tell you that children who cry and throw tantrums in protest at the parent who is leaving them in the hands of strangers will usually within minutes settle down and begin happily going about painting or hammering—or listening to the teacher *after* the parents leave.

In the first sentence of the book of Isaiah, the prophet says, "In the year that King Uzziah died, I saw the Lord."— Isaiah 6:1. While he might have meant the sentence to be a chronological reference, what it also says to me is that while the king was still alive, Isaiah *didn't* fully see the Lord.

It is both the mystery and challenge of the Christian faith to love and serve a God who, in the physical sense, "left" us. Yes, we were given the gift of the Holy Spirit as Guide and Comforter, and yes we can sense that God is in and all around us. Yet haven't each of us at one time or another felt like the little girl who was whimpering in the darkness after having had a bad dream? Her mother came in and comforted her, and told her not to be afraid, because God was watching out for her. "I know he is, Mommy," she said through her sniffling, "but sometimes I just need God with skin on."

I once had the privilege of being escorted to a speaking engagement by a young minister from Russia. He had read the book *Jesus, CEO,* and said that many of the thoughts in the book had challenged him. I likewise found some of his interpretations of scripture interesting, as well. He said, "My friends sometimes ask, 'Uri, why isn't God answering my prayer? Why isn't he taking this problem away from me?' And you know what I tell them, Laurie?" he stated, waving his hands dramatically as he also maneuvered us through traffic. "I tell them—'That's easy, you idiot! He doesn't answer your prayer because he wants you to grow up! He is tired of baby-sitting! Maybe he is waiting for *you* to become the son or daughter who will make him proud! Quit asking for relief and start showing some belief!' " He laughed joyously as we made the next turn.

God has released us so we can grow.

"Greater things than I have done shall you also do." Jesus said.—John 14:12. (But you cannot do it until I am gone.)

Michelangelo's poignant rendering of the creation shows God's outstretched hand releasing Adam to the world. Two outstretched hands, only inches apart, so aptly describe our relationship to God . . . so close . . . yet so far away.

In reading accounts of near-death experiences I find it amazing that even mothers with young children reported experiencing a presence of love so intense that they did not want to return to earth. They were so immersed and saturated with a sense of peace that even leaving a child was almost not an issue.

How could Jesus leave us if he loved us so much? Because he knew the Comforter would come . . . he knew we would grow into the fullness of God individually, as he had.

"Father, I give them back to You."—John 17:11

He knew the power of release.

Question

Could there be any possible advantages to Jesus' physically "leaving" us?

Question

Name a time when you performed better when your parent or mentor was not physically present.

Question

When Jesus left, did he really go? If not, how and where does he still remain present today?

Power Connection:

Dear Lord, help me release others to You and Your Holy Spirit, so that they can grow in Your light rather than suffer in my shadow.

Amen.

I,_____, know the power of release.

Perspective

"If your eye is sound, your whole body will be full of light."
—Matthew 6:22

perspective: 1. a technique of depicting volumes and spatial relationships on a flat surface 2. a visible scene, especially one extending to a distance; vista 3. the manner in which objects appear to the eye in respect to their relative positions and distance 4. one's mental view of facts, ideas, etc., and their interrelationships 5. the ability to see all the relevant data in a meaningful relationship
(*Random House Webster's College Dictionary*)

"To have a friend is to live two lives." So read the quote in a greeting card I once bought, no author credited with the words. I have since pondered that saying. If having a friend is living two lives, then being a friend of God gives us the perspective of living, and loving, many lives.

Perspective means viewing a situation in a certain way. Once we begin to see things the way Jesus did, our world views will change. We begin to perceive situations not through our eyes only, but also through his. Compassion and empathy must become innate qualities. Fearlessness and faith must be our natural response to challenges.

To have a friend is to live two lives.

What an awesome invitation we have been given—to come and live with God—to come and be his friend. To see the world through his eyes. To gain a new perspective.

He Knew God
Draws in Circles

My art director friend, Siegfried, once created a three-panel photo card for me. The first panel showed Einstein at the blackboard, drawing a small circle. The next showed him drawing a larger circle extending out from the first one, and the third panel showed him drawing circles so large they extended past the limits of the blackboard. All the circles were connected, each spiraling out from the other, beginning with the circle of the smallest atom and expanding to the spirals of the galaxies. I love that card because it reminds me of God at work—drawing in circles.

When the Scribes and the Pharisees brought the woman taken in adultery to Jesus for judgment, he knelt down and began to draw in the sand. I'm convinced he did not draw a straight line, demarcating "On this side are the sinners—on this side are the saints." He said, "Whoever is without sin among you may cast the first stone," and then he began to draw in circles—circles that took in all their sins—circles that surrounded all of them with love.—John 7:8

What goes around, comes around. When we dispense mercy, we receive mercy. When we give value, we receive value in return. "As you have done, so will it be done to you; your deeds will recoil on your own head." —Obadiah 1:15

The new theory in physics is that the building blocks of the universe are not "blocks" at all, but rather loops that spiral in ten dimensions.

Every encounter you have with someone, whether it is your neighbor or the clerk at the grocery store or your associates at work, will come back to you, enlarged. The ancient Indians knew this truth when they drew sacred spirals in the sand, around and around and around. The earth spins in a circle. The blood flows through our bodies in circulations of return.

I get amused at all the graphs people use to chart progress. We have such a linear mentality in our work, always focused on the *bottom line*. We like to see horizontals and verticals— especially verticals, always shooting higher and higher, showing our profits going up and up. Yet life is composed of seasons and cycles, spirals rather than verticals.

People of perspective know that what goes up, will come down, and that the tide that surges will also ebb. Wisdom means being aware of the balances in Nature, and always leaving room for the circle to return.

When we have perspective, we are acknowledging that God is at work, drawing in circles we can't always see. Psalm 30:5 reads "Weeping may endure for a night, but joy cometh in the morning." Knowing this, we can have faith when things seem to be the darkest. The sun will circle around again, and joy will return.

The Old Testament recounts the story of Jacob, a man who was a renowned trickster. Taking advantage of his aged and nearly blind father, Jacob covers his arms with goat's hair so he will resemble his hairy brother, Esau. He uses this ruse to trick his dad into giving him a blessing that traditionally went to the eldest son, who is, in this case, Esau. Jacob escapes from an angry Esau after the trick is discovered, and in his exile Jacob falls in love with the daughter of his uncle, Laban. So smitten is he with her that he promises to work seven years for free in exchange for Rebecca. On the wedding night, Jacob gets drunk and awakens to find himself married to Leah, Rebecca's older sister. Uncle Laban has tricked him, and Jacob has to work another seven years for Rebecca's hand.—Genesis 25–27, 29

What goes around, comes around. Jacob the trickster got tricked.

Henry Wadsworth Longfellow wrote, "The universe is an immeasurable wheel, turning forever more . . . revealing with each pass things unseen before" ("Rain in Summer").

King David knew in his own life that God drew in circles. Perhaps that is why he wrote the following beautiful verses.

"They went away, went away weeping, carrying their seed.
They come back, come back singing, carrying their sheaves."
—PSALM 126:6

Jesus knew God draws in circles.

Question

How has God drawn in circles in your life?

Question

Do you see yourself being on a vertical chart, or rather in an ever-ascending spiral?

Question

What are you putting out that will come back around to you enlarged?

Question

How can knowing God draws in circles make you more visionary?

Power Connection:

Dear Lord, help me remember that what I give, I will receive back multiplied. Help me trust You to do Your work on my behalf, always drawing in circles guaranteed for the highest good.

Amen.

I, _____, know God draws in circles.

He Had a Larger Perspective

When Jesus said, "I have sheep in another fold which I also must gather,"—John 10:16, he was indicating to us that he was not focusing on the perspective of this world alone. He was looking at the Big Picture from day one—not just at what was going on that day in Jerusalem. A leader must view things from a larger perspective. I am reminded of the intellectual who was asked how he enjoyed a party of rather narrow-minded guests. His comment was "It was fascinating. Every viewpoint from A to B was represented."

We have to stretch our base of knowledge, information, and influence in order to be effective. Yet so often we surround ourselves with people who look and think and act like we do. While this may add to our comfort level, it does little to bring about new awareness or stimulate original ideas.

Faith Popcorn, the futurist who is highly paid for her

Think Tank's prediction of trends, does not make forecasts merely by sitting around reading the *Wall Street Journal*. She and her group research and seek out the fringes of society. Futurists stretch their perspective by listening to rap music, or any type that is a radical departure from "the norm." They might read *Mother Earth* magazine, *Science Digest,* and other periodicals that have no apparent relevance to their current fields of endeavor. They seek the edges, because it is the edges that ultimately lead us. A wise person does not fear the edges and fringes, but studies them. Indeed, he or she is often *in* them—working to make change happen.

Renaissance painters needed very large frames for their pictures, because the scenes they depicted often included hosts of angels looking down on the subjects. Perhaps this larger perspective on life is what helped them to emerge from the Dark Ages. They made room for the heavenly hosts in their frames of reference.

USA Today recently reported that the city of Boston had no juvenile homicide over a ten-month period, compared to sixteen homicides the year before. Apparently the drop in the death rate was due to the larger perspective the new police commissioner and the citizens took. One of the first moves the commissioner, Paul Evans, made in his new job was to meet with the anti-gang unit. "I fully expected them to tell me we needed more cops, tougher judges, and more jail space," says Evans. Instead they said, "We need more jobs and alternative activities for these kids."

So Evans and the police began meeting with citizens in the neighborhood and local business leaders to address the problems. Funds were raised to provide programming and memberships to Boys and Girls Clubs and the YMCA. Job training and skills programs were created. And as a result, not one youth died during that ten-month period. They lived because people finally looked at the problem from a larger perspective.

Jesus was looking far beyond the shores of Galilee when he prayed. He was praying into the future—into the needs of the ghettos and the gangs as well as the prostitutes and tax collectors and fishermen. He spent time seeking the big picture, making room for heaven in his frame of reference.

"I am not praying for these alone, but also for those in the future"—John 17:20

Jesus had a larger perspective.

Question

Do you shun and/or ignore viewpoints that are radically different from yours?

Question

If so, what could this narrow focus be costing you?

Question

How far can you see from where you sit?

Question

How far do you really look?

Question

Do you leave room for heaven in your frame?

Power Connection:

Dear Lord, help me remember that I am part of a small area in a young country on a planet that is but a tiny blue dot in space. Help me daily to stretch my imagination and my boundaries. Help me go to the edges of my immediate problem and ponder what lies beyond. Help me keep a larger perspective and think of others' needs.

Amen.

I, _____, have a larger perspective.

He Knew That Moving Isn't Fun

Recently I decided to relocate—again. During this time I got discouraged and overwhelmed and began to question why I was even in business, much less why I was once again moving all traces of it. (My mother now writes my address only in pencil.) As I sat surrounded by stacks and piles of unpacked "miscellaneous" items, I received a card in the mail from my friend Catherine. It read, "Don't get discouraged, Laurie. Even movers know that moving is not fun."

Yet a leader's main job is, frankly, to get people to move. Jesus' job was to get people to move—from a state of sin to a state of grace, from a world of bondage to a world of freedom, from a state of tears to one of everlasting joy. This was no easy task, because Jesus quickly encountered the fact that a body in motion tends to stay in motion, while a body at rest TENDS TO STAY AT REST.

In the Old Testament, Abraham earned God's blessing,

even though his story proves that moving isn't fun. After the death of Abraham's father, God told him, "Leave your own country behind you, and your own people, and go to the land I will guide you to."—Genesis 12:1

Abraham's move involved packing up his family (at the age of seventy-five), and heading into enemy territory. Along the way he encountered famine—Genesis 12:10, a forced departure with an armed escort—Genesis 12:20, a battle among asphalt pits—Genesis 14:10–15, and a near death encounter in Sodom and Gomorrah—Genesis 19:27. On none of these occasions was he given a senior citizen's discount.

Moses, too, learned the hard lesson about getting people to move. At an age when others were thinking about retirement, Moses had to think about the logistics involved in getting the entire Israelite nation out of Egypt. (Perhaps one reason it took that group forty years to make an eleven-day journey was that they were still packing when the moving camels arrived.)

Inertia, when first confronted, appears to be an immovable force. We are creatures who like comfort, patterns, and repetition. "This is the way we've always done it." "I've invested fifteen years in this relationship or project or job, and you're telling me it's time to change?" "If God had wanted us to _____ He would have given us _____." (You fill in the blanks.) We do not like change.

Yet change is life's only constant. One of Catherine's favorite cartoons shows a man and his wife on back of a camel, trudging through the desert. The wife keeps asking, "Are we there yet? Are we there yet?" Until finally the man turns to her and says, "We will never be *there*, Dear. We're *nomads*, remember?" When we choose to become God's people, we are, in effect, becoming nomads, ready to move at a moment's calling, knowing this earth is not our home, and God's breath is a wind ever changing.

I recently wrote a poem for a friend who was confronting a painful change in her life. At one point as we were talking she sighed, "I just thought I would have it all together by now." But now she was hearing an insistent inner voice telling her it was time to move.

CHANGE

Expanding . . . contracting . . .
breathing out . . . breathing in . . .
Life is about change
in the midst of constancy.
We go to the Fair. We watch horses run.
And in the midst of our laughter
and whispered fears
sits a statue

at the foot of your stairs
who seems to have it all
together.
And yet somehow
she envies us—
our laughter
and our chaos
as we run
up the stairs . . .
to
meet, embrace, and dance again
with "change."

If we are alive and breathing, there is probably an inner voice telling us to move—to move up and out to help somebody, to move to make amends, to move toward the art we feel inside—to move toward our destiny.

"You have stayed long enough on this mountain. Move on from here—continue your journey." —Deuteronomy 1:6–8

Jesus warned his followers: "You must be ready for me when I call you, no matter what the hour."—Matthew 25:13

Jesus knew that moving isn't fun.

Question

What move do you need to make right now?

Question

Knowing that moving isn't fun, what are the rewards that nevertheless await you?

Power Connection:

Dear Lord,

It is Your nature to have Your people be continually moving—ever onward, ever upward, from glory to glory. It is the in-between times that seem so difficult. Help me to make the move I know I must, even if it will not be "fun." I, too, desire to enter into the land of blessing that awaits—just on the other side of this deep, deep valley.

Amen

I, _____, know that moving isn't fun.

He Was Not Attached to Form

In the Old Testament the Israelites are warned, "Since you saw no shape on that day when Yahweh spoke to you from the midst of the fire, take care! And see that you do not make yourself a carved image *in the shape of anything at all.*" —Deuteronomy 4:16

Unfortunately, they didn't heed the warning. "They made a calf at Horeb, performing prostration to a smelted thing, exchanging the One who was their glory for the image of a grass-eating ox." —Psalm 106:19. The Israelites were like any of us who decide that in order to feel secure we have to worship some form that we can see and touch. Our fears and insecurities can all too easily attach themselves to golden calves. If we are afraid of being poor, "money" becomes the idol we worship. If we are afraid of failure, "success" becomes the golden calf. If we are afraid of being alone, a relationship becomes the god. Looking at the wars and bloodshed that have taken place throughout history between the Christians and pagans, the Muslims and the Jews, the Catholics and the Protestants, one could say we have even made golden calves of our "religions" and denominations, and forgotten the One True God.

Jesus was not attached to the form of things—even his own physical body. He was not heavily invested in the forms of physical matter at all, even when it seemed to be in a state of death or decay. "But, Master, he stinketh!" they warned when he began to call forth a man who had been three days in the tomb.—John 11:38. Wouldn't it have been easier to raise up someone a little more "freshly dead"? Jesus knew that all form was temporary and relative. "Quake, earth, at the coming of your Master, at the coming of the God of Jacob, who turns rock into pool, and flint into fountain." — Psalm 114:7–8

Often we think a relationship or project should turn out a certain way, but, if we are wise, we must be willing to have it take another form.

Two of my friends in San Diego run a very successful gift and garden shop. For more than twenty years they had been located in a choice part of Old Town, when despite their best efforts, they lost their lease. Depressed and discouraged, they decided to move to a smaller town, certain that by losing their location they had lost their business. Within a year, however, they were offered a lease in a location in San Diego right off the freeway, which had even greater visibility—and better parking—than their former location. They seized the opportunity, and today their store is stronger than ever. They admit that they had gotten so attached to the physical location of their business that they had overlooked the spirit of it, which is really what their customers had been responding to all along.

Many projects or inventions that start out as one thing end up as something else. People who are too attached to the form of things are locking themselves into "realities" that are almost always sure to change. A leader looks for the spirit of a project and is aware that its physical manifestation may take many shapes.

This also pertains to the form and concept of "family." When told that his family was looking for him, Jesus said his family was not the one born of blood, but by choice. "My family is the one who does the will of God."—Matthew 12:46–50. I have known people whose blood relatives were miserable, wounded souls but who had been given, through God's grace, friends or mentors who took over the nurturing process, and became families of choice. "He lifts the needy out of their misery, and gives them a flock of new families; at the sight of which, upright hearts rejoice." —Psalm 107:41

God is not attached to form. His original choice for the first king of Israel was a tall and handsome man named Saul. Saul, however, proved to be incapable of leading. God then searched out *another* man named David and prepared him for the throne. God changed the form to a new, more responsive leader, one who was not going to rule in the old, domineering ways.—1 Samuel 15:17–28

When I was being interviewed on the book tour for *The Path*, I was the guest of a black radio talk-show host who somewhat angrily introduced me as "Laurie Beth Jones, a white woman." He continued, "I don't know why any of my brothers and sisters should listen to a white woman, but here she is. Say something, Ms. Jones." I took a deep breath and then said, "Yes, I am a white woman. But I assure you this form is temporary." There was a long silence, and then he smiled. "You're right. Begin."

"There is neither Jew nor Greek, slave nor free, male nor female, for you are all one in Christ Jesus." —Galatians 3:28

Jesus was not attached to form.

Question

What physical forms are you attached to?
- in your relationships?
- your work?
- your daily living?

Question

What would happen if you didn't view yourself as a body? What form would you be?

Power Connection:

Dear Lord, I am so prone to get attached to the form of things, I easily forget that everything lives and breathes and moves only through Your grace and will. Help me stay flexible and aware that You are God, and that You can easily change the forms in my life, without harming the spirit in it.

Amen.

I, _____, do not get attached to form.

He Stood in the Gap

There is an incredible painting by the Spanish artist Sorolla that depicts a man dressed in a priestly white gown standing before a group of lepers. His arms are raised, and the expression on his face is a mixture of anger and compassion. He faces a crowd of children which is ready to hurl sticks and rocks at the lepers huddled behind him. The priest stands in the gap as a human shield. In another of his works, Sorolla painted a black-robed priest wading in the water. He is surrounded by three children who have left their crutches on the shore. He is helping one of the little boys to learn how to float. Again the priest is standing in the gap—helping children feel power*ful* instead of power*less*. In each case it is a human being who is standing in the gap. In Ecclesiasticus, there is an impressive list of leaders and their accomplishments. Among them is Phinehas, who stood firm when the people revolted. "Phinehas son of Eleazar is third in glory because of his zeal in the fear of the Lord. Because he stood firm when the people revolted; with a staunch and courageous heart; he made expiation for Israel."—Ecclesiasticus 45:23–24 (*New Jerusalem Bible*). His stance of faith filled in the gap for an entire nation.

Jesus stood in the gap for us. He was willing to come up against all the negative forces in the world and tell us, in effect, "Get behind me and they cannot affect you. I will absorb and deflect the harm." A person of perspective has to be willing to stand in the gap—the gap between someone who understands the vision for the future and someone who doesn't, the gap between someone who thinks the dollar is almighty and someone who knows it is a side effect, between someone who has only short-term thinking and someone who knows that seeds must be planted and cultivated and then harvested down the line.

One of my closest friends and associates is a man who is attempting to implement major changes in health care—particularly for the elderly. He must regularly stand in the gap between the deep, human needs of the people his company serves and the highly profit-oriented demands of Wall Street. The two groups speak different vocabularies and have an almost entirely different set of needs and goals. Yet unless someone like this CEO stands in the gap (and is willing to sometimes be torn limb from limb by either camp), the needs of either group will not be met. He is willing to stand in the gap.

I recently met a dance teacher from St. Paul–Minneapolis, who shared with me that her young dream had been to dance on Broadway. Faced with the choice of dancing in New York or getting married in Minneapolis, she listened to her family and friends and decided the safer route of marriage was best. She said, "That choice has haunted me for twenty years." She now has four students who have won scholarships to dance on Broadway, each of them being chosen from a field of thousands. It seems that one particular young student of hers has scoliosis, which will ultimately require a steel rod being placed in her back, ending her career. She said, "My student curled up like a baby, weeping as I held her, fearing her parents would now stop her from dancing." This teacher, after consulting with experts who agreed the surgery could be delayed several years, finally persuaded the girl's concerned parents to let her continue dancing. This student won one of the dance scholarships. The girl's dream came true, thanks to one woman who was willing to stand in the gap for her, (as she wished someone had done for her twenty years before.)

Youth advocates who work in the court system stand in the gap for the young people they represent. Day-care workers stand in the gap for parents who can't be with their children while they work. Lawyers who work pro bono for clients who need justice but can't afford the court costs stand in the gap. Soldiers who put themselves in harm's way so poor people can receive humanitarian aid stand in the gap. I have a friend who flew in from out of town to attend a young girl's graduation because the student's mother had died from AIDS the year before. "I came to stand here for her mother," she explained as the ceremonial march began. Big Brothers and Big Sisters stand in the gap for kids who need role models in a harsh and frightening world. I believe that each of us is called to stand in the gap for one another.

"The Lord said to Ezekiel: I sought for anyone among them who would repair the wall and stand in the breach before me."—Ezekiel 22:30

Jesus stood in the gap.

Question

Where do you need to place yourself to fill in a gap?

Question

What will be the costs—and benefits—of your doing that?

Power Connection:

Dear Lord, help me stand in the gap for others. Help me be the bridge across which others can run to their dreams.

Amen.

I, _____, stand in the gap.

He Kept It Precious

When Moses came down from the mountain, almost every commandment he was given was designed "to keep it precious."

Thou shalt not take the name of the Lord thy God in vain—Keep it precious.

Remember the sabbath—Keep this day precious.

Honor your father and mother—Keep them precious.

Thou shalt not kill—Keep life precious.

Thou shalt not commit adultery—Keep the marriage vows precious.

Every commandment instructing us not to lie, cheat, or steal is really about keeping truth, honor, and respect for God and one another precious.

Our society is reeling with crimes of hatred, neglect, and violence because we have failed to keep the holy things precious. The temples that are our bodies, the kingdoms that are our minds, the altars that are our hearts, the portals that are our mouths, the gates that are our eyes—we have too often failed to keep them precious. Instead we have undervalued and misused and abused them. In many ways we have become the pigs trampling pearls.

When Jesus turned over the moneychangers' tables, he was keeping God's name precious. When he healed the little girl, he was keeping life precious. When he lifted his cup and broke the bread and said, "Do this in remembrance of me," he was keeping the memories of all the times they'd laughed and cried and shared precious. And when he willingly spilled his blood upon the ground, he was keeping it precious. All of it. All of us.

Ham, one of the sons of Noah, was cursed because he stared at his father's nakedness. "And Noah began to be an husbandman, and he planted a vineyard. And he drank of the wine, and was drunken; and he was uncovered within his tent. And Ham, the father of Canaan, saw the nakedness of his father, and told his two brethren without. And Shem and Japheth took a garment and laid it upon both their shoulders, and went backward, and covered the nakedness of their father; and their faces were backward, and they saw not their father's nakedness. And Noah awoke from his wine, and knew what his younger son had done unto him." —Genesis 9:20–24. Ham received harsh punishment because he had failed to respect his father's dignity. He failed to keep it precious.

The priest asked the name of the child as the parents brought her forward for baptism. He lifted her up and sprinkled a few drops of water on her head. As he lit a candle to denote her new life, a breeze came through the church and the tiny flame began to sputter. Immediately, her father rushed forward and cupped his hands around the flame, hovering over it until it was strong enough to have his hands drawn away. A new life is such a precious tiny flame—and we, too, must all of us—cup our hands around it until it grows strong enough to give light on its own.

"I am Yahweh, your God, the Holy One of Israel, your savior. Because you are precious in my eyes, because you are honored and I love you, I give men in exchange for you, peoples in return for your life." —Isaiah 43:3–5

Jesus kept it precious.

Question

What is the "it" you must keep precious?

Question

What treasures do you see being trampled upon?
• in your home?
• your workplace?
• society?

Question

What can you do to keep holy things precious?

Power Connection:

Dear Lord, help me to see what I must keep precious. Give me discerning eyes, a willing heart, and a ready mind to restore what has been laid waste. Help me keep all that is holy precious.

Amen.

I, _____, keep it precious.

He Made a Covenant
with the Present

A covenant is a sacred promise or agreement. Often in our daily actions and decision making we are not establishing an agreement with the present but merely reliving old habits from the past. Authors and psychologists have long documented how all too frequently "the sins of the fathers are visited upon the next generation." We can easily and thoroughly imprint, and thus imbed, programming that does not serve us. The mind, like a video recorder, simply records. It does not edit unless *consciously* directed to do so. Many people find themselves saying or doing the very same things that they most hated about their parents, because their unedited minds have somehow made a "covenant with the past."

In Isaiah 48:6–7, God tells a stubborn people, "Now I am revealing *new* things to you—things hidden and unknown to you, created *just now, this very moment* . . . of these things you have heard nothing until now, so that you cannot say, 'Oh yes, I knew all this.' " In Jeremiah 31:31–33, God says, "I am making a *new* covenant with you—not like the covenant I made with your fathers. No—*this one is with you.*"

Jesus came to make a new covenant—to close the door on the past and set up a new order. And to enable it to happen, he had to make a covenant with the present.

One of the sayings that most comforts me when I go into a state of stress is "I am always safe in the moment." When I am stressed it is nearly always because I am dealing with the "what if's" of the future or the "if only's" of the past. Jesus made a covenant with the present because he knew that is where true power resides—in the perfect moment of the here and now. God is I AM that I AM. Not I USED TO BE or I'M GOING BE. The only power we have is in the present.

All the power of the universe is hovering around us— waiting for us to claim it and call it forth into being. Just because we have stumbled for years in the dark doesn't mean we can't, or shouldn't, turn on the light. When Jesus constantly declared, "In the past it was written . . . BUT I SAY . . ." he was declaring his covenant with the present, and thus with a new future, built upon a new relationship with God.

Author Lynne Andrews offers a powerful exercise for workshop participants. They are asked to write down their past failures and mistakes on a piece of paper, and then burn it publicly. They then drive a stake in the ground to denote the present. "Here, my new power begins. Here, I take a stand." When Isaiah exhorted the Israelites to expand their territories, he reminded them to make their "tent pegs firm." In other words, this is here and now.

In one of the exercises from my book *The Path: Creating Your Mission Statement for Work and Life*, I ask people to visualize their family members, living or dead, standing with them in a room. I ask them to see each person, one by one, coming forward to present them with a gift. Then I ask them to repeat the visualization, except this time each person is carrying a cup of sorrow. "Each person in your past was probably drinking from a cup of sorrow. Look in the cup and see what's in it—what event or circumstance caused each of them disappointment or pain?"

One woman in particular saw her mother coming forward, offering her a cup filled with the ingredients of bitterness and negativity. I role-played the part of her mother and said to her, "People cannot be trusted. Life is full of pain, Joyce. This is how it is." I offered her the cup, saying, "Will you drink my cup with me?" Joyce looked at me/her mother and said, "Mom, it's taken me twenty years of therapy to come to this point, and I do love you, but I will not drink from that cup anymore." She took a deep breath, and with a trembling hand, she pushed the cup away.

Jesus drank the cup of sorrow once and for all. We do not

have to drink from the cup of the past. We can, each of us, right now, begin a covenant with the *present*.

Another of his disciples said, "Sir, when my father is dead then I will follow you." But Jesus told him "Follow me *now*. Let those who are spiritually dead care for their own dead." —Matthew 8:21–22. Let the past bury the past.

Jesus made a covenant with the present.

Question

What covenants with the past have been holding you back?

Question

What past "cups of sorrow" have been your beverage of choice?

Question

How can you physically declare a new covenant with the present?

Question

Write out your personal, individualized covenant with the present.

Power Connection:

Dear Lord, help me make sacred vows in the here and now, relinquishing all my past disappointments and failures. Here, I take a stand. Here, is holy ground. I know and claim Your power, now, in this very moment.

Amen.

I, _____, make a covenant with the present.

He Carried the Right Lesson Forward

Management consultant Peter Senge defines a learning disability as the tendency to take the wrong lesson away from an event or situation. For example, a child learning to ride a bike falls down and carries away the lesson that she needs to pedal faster, whereas an adult suffering the same mishap might take forward the "lesson" that she is uncoordinated and is therefore a failure. In this case, both activities were the same—falling down—but the child learned the right lesson and the adult the wrong one. Hence, the adult had a "learning disability." When Peter formerly known as Simon denied Jesus three times, most of us would have "fired" him. But Jesus took the right lesson forward of appreciating the value of a deeply repentant—and more willing—heart.

Confrontations at home and in the workplace occur every day, with many people learning the wrong lessons from them. For example, rather than concluding about a trying coworker that "Jim is just a jerk," a better lesson might be, "Jim is the sandpaper God is using to finish me to perfection." Whenever there is blame and finger-pointing, rather than inner reflection and a search for solutions, the wrong lessons are being carried forward.

A second marriage is often described as "the triumph of hope over experience." People who marry again are choosing to learn positive lessons from their former relationships and move forward.

Sometimes a narrow perspective causes the wrong lesson to be advanced.

What can be drawn from the following scenario? A publicly traded nursing home company recently sold three of its facilities and made a five-million-dollar return on its investments. Yet I personally toured some of the facilities immediately after the sale and saw where human needs of the residents had gone unmet in pursuit of greater profits. For example, the lobby of each facility had been repainted, carpeted, and professionally decorated to increase its "floor appeal." Yet upstairs, where the residents lived, no improvements had been made. In fact, there weren't even blinds or shades on the windows in many of the rooms because, as the supervisor explained, "We were told we had to cut costs in order to increase our bottom line." The residents were even gathering at the nurses' station because there was no recreation area they could use. The garden was off limits to them, "to keep it clean and to help keep maintenance costs down." I'm sure the investors were very satisfied with their dollar-per-dollar return. Yet I wonder how many of them knew what frail and elderly people had to do without so the shareholders could multiply their earnings. In my opinion, to define that kind of profit-taking as a "successful investment" is taking the wrong lesson forward.

Sometimes in life a minor setback can lead to the wrong lesson being learned. For example, Mary's five-year-old nephew Christopher couldn't wait for Halloween. He got his costume ready weeks in advance, excitedly discussing all the candy he was going to get. Yet when the evening arrived, the first house he and his mother approached happened to be the home of one of those guys who love to scare kids. This man opened the door suddenly and, dressed in a black Dracula costume, gave a hideously frightening and evil laugh. Christopher backed up so quickly that he nearly knocked his mother down. Not one to show fear overtly (being male acculturated even at that early age), he looked quickly in his sack and said, "Mom, I think I have enough candy now. Let's go." When they went home and the doorbell rang, Christopher said, "I'll get it!" He opened the door and then proceeded to dump the entire bowl of candy in the sack of the trick-or-treater at their door. "There—that's finished!" he exclaimed as he closed the door and turned out the light. And that was his

Halloween. Much more fun awaited Christopher had he continued down the block. But he let that first phony Dracula send him scurrying home. Christopher, like many of us, was taking the wrong lesson forward.

Whenever an event causes us to shrink back and be afraid or feel disempowered, chances are we are taking the wrong lesson forward. The mind is constantly forming conclusions, and in a world saturated with negative messages, it is too easy to stamp a lesson with a message of fear.

Jacob, only eighteen months old, was running around in delight at the birthday party, grabbing big red balloons and hugging them to his chest like his older brother Joseph. Suddenly the balloon he was holding popped with a loud bang. Jacob's eyes grew wide and he quickly searched the crowd for the face of his mother, his lower lip beginning to quiver in preparation for a loud wail. But his mother laughed and clapped her hands, as did three-year-old Joseph. "Hurray, Jacob, hurray!" she called out. "That was funny!" Jacob's lips slowly turned into a smile as he, too, clapped his hands. Her example of laughing at surprises taught him, in that instant, to be less afraid of change. Jacob's mother showed him how to carry the right lesson forward.

If only each of us lived and worked in such an atmosphere. One thing we could all resolve to do is to help each other to laugh, not cry, when a big red balloon suddenly bursts in our arms. There will always be other balloons (or jobs, or people) to hold. That is the lesson to carry forward.

Jesus did not let fear dictate his activities. He took the consistent message of God's love as being the right lesson to take forward. He declared *love* to be the foundation of all he stood for rather than *fear*, and triumph, not failure.

"Then Peter said to Jesus, 'Lord, how many times shall I forgive my brother when he sins against me? Up to seven times?' Jesus answered, "I tell you not seven times, but seventy times seven."—Matthew 18:22

Jesus carried the right lesson forward.

Question

When in your life have you let the first phony Dracula send you running home?

Question

What are some clues that "learning disabilities" are occurring:
- in your family?
- in your workplace?
- in your community?

Question

What could be the right lesson to take forward from your most recent setback?

Power Connection:

Dear Lord, in every situation where I feel hurt or upset, let me be sure to take the right lesson forward. Help me know that in You, with You, and because of You, every lesson is a valuable one and only comes from love. Keep me always searching for the next bright red balloon.

Amen.

I, _____, take the right lesson forward.

He Recognized True Worth

Recently I attended a horse auction in New Mexico. I went early to talk to the owners, check out the horses, and even ride one or two before the auction began. It is not unusual for the most desirable horses to be sold before the actual bidding takes place. As I walked by the corrals, I overheard one rancher bragging to his buddies that he had gotten the full asking price of $2,500 for his two-year-old filly—selling her to some kid before the auction even started. The rancher fell gloomily silent, however, when one hour later that same "kid" ran the filly through the same auction and sold her for $4,200. Clearly, the rancher had not recognized his horse's true worth.

Jesus recognized true worth. When Jesus looked at Mary Magdalene, he did not see an adulteress, but a human being capable of profound love. When he looked at Peter, he did not see a fisherman, but a leader of tremendous potential and power. When he looked at people, he did not see them as defined by their labels or their job descriptions—he recognized their true worth. How did he appraise their true worth? "Man judges by appearances, but God looks on the heart."—1 Samuel 16:7

One aspect of business is knowing the true worth of a product or service and marketing it at the appropriate price. If businesspeople do not know the true value of their product or services, they will quickly go out of business.

We all remember the story of the goose that laid golden eggs. The foolish farmer who owned her thought the eggs were more valuable than the goose that laid them. He got hungry one day and ate the goose, thinking he could live forever on the income produced by the few golden eggs he already had. This parable reminds me of some corporate executives who lay off valuable employees to inflate the bottom line. Typically, to fill in the gap they later have to bring in consultants who charge five to six times what the original employees were making.

I remember once having a disturbing dream in which I was negotiating a price for an idea that I had. The clients offered a sum, which I accepted. I then woke up, literally, in a sweat, realizing, "My idea was worth a lot more than that! I undersold myself!" The terror was not that I had foolishly left money on the table (aargh!), but more importantly that I had failed to recognize the true worth of an idea.

When Jesus preached about the merchant who sold everything he had to buy one pearl, he was teaching about recognizing true worth. History tells of Saint Lawrence, a humble priest who happened to be captured by one of the many bands that attacked villages and towns in the third century. Wanting money, his captors demanded that he bring out the treasures of the church. He quietly went about the village and gathered up the children and the elderly, the frail and the infirm. "These are the treasures of the church," he said, "but you can have the gold."

Young Perceval, the earnest knight who set out to find the Holy Grail, was invited to a banquet in a mighty hall. Immediately following the banquet the angry king threw him in prison. "Why—what have I done?" Perceval asked as they hurled him into the dungeon. "The grail was placed before you three times last night, and you failed to recognize it," said the angry king. Perceval learned a painful lesson about not seeing the treasures that exist under our very noses.

"Stop judging by mere appearances, and make a *right* judgement."—John 7:24

Jesus recognized true worth.

Question

What are you undervaluing:
• in your workplace?
• in your relationships?
• in your life?

Question

How can you learn to appraise things at their true worth?

Power Connection:

Dear Lord, help me value what You value. Help me see the truth worth—in every person and in every situation. Let me see the diamond hidden in the coal, and the hopeful heart behind a pair of downcast eyes. Let me see Your treasures, as You see them.

Amen.

I, _____, recognize true worth.

He Brought Them
into Remembrance

When Moses was leading the Israelites across the wilderness he often had to remind them of the slavery and harsh realities of the life they left behind in order to keep them moving forward. "Remember that you were slaves in Egypt, and the Lord your God brought you out with a great display of miracles." —Deuteronomy 15:5

David brought to remembrance the many battles he had won over the former predators of his flocks before he hurled the stone that killed the giant Goliath. The prophet Isaiah's duty was to call people to remembrance—of who they were and of their glorious destiny. "Remember, O Israel, that you are God's servant. He made you, and will not forget you." —Isaiah 44:21

One of the most powerful steps a leader can take is to call people to remembrance—of past victories, of glorious moments, of days when the cup was full, when promises were made and kept. Nehemiah was a master at this—summoning the Jews together so that Ezra the scribe could recite the Law and remind them of their heritage. "Ezra the scribe stood on a wooden dais erected for this purpose, and began to read the law. After hearing the law, and realizing how far away from it they had gotten, the people wept for days." —Nehemiah 8:4. As a result of this formal ceremony the Jews not only began to rebuild the walls of Jerusalem, but also reformed their ways. Nehemiah had "brought them into remembrance."

God himself is described as having a Book of Remembrance. "And he had a Book of Remembrance drawn up in which he recorded the names of those who loved to think about him." —Malachi 3:16

When Jesus stood and calmly asked the angry crowd to cast the first stone—if they could—against the woman taken in adultery, he was calling each of them into the remembrance of their own shortcomings and sins. When he spoke the words of Isaiah to describe what he had been called upon to accomplish, he was bringing people into remembrance of words they had all learned as children, but perhaps had forgotten in their daily rush for living and surviving under harsh Roman rule. "Remember that God will give beauty for ashes, joy instead of mourning, praise instead of heaviness. Remember your God." —Isaiah 41:3

Whenever it seemed that the Israelites were poised at the gate of change, God sent someone to bring them into remembrance of all the times God had helped them in the past.

The word *remember* is mentioned more than 250 times in Scripture. Clearly, many times it is not new knowledge that we need, but reminders of what we already know.

Sports psychologists claim that by remembering when athletes do something *right,* they can easily duplicate those activities over and over. They emphasize remembering past successes in order to attain new ones. Sometimes we need to look backward in order to move forward. The inscription on a government building in Washington, D.C., reads: "What is past, is prologue."

David said he wanted the law of the Lord to be always on his lips, so that he could constantly remember his God. A famous American poet said, "Our birth is both a sleep and a forgetting . . ." Can it be that we have forgotten who we are? Did Jesus come to re-"mind" us that we have a glorious heritage—and deep responsibility—to love God and one another? "Do this *in remembrance* of me." —Luke 22:19

The city of Orlando was able to defeat zoning ordinances that would have brought adult bookstores and strip clubs into the heart of downtown. Unwilling to admit defeat, the "girlie show" businessowners decided to approach the rural surrounding areas—where the opposition might be less vociferous. Hearing of their plan to move to an outlying town, the mayor of Orlando went to their town council meeting and asked for a chance to speak. She stood up and reminded the council members of the well-known and respected writers, doctors, teachers, and ministers who had come from that town. She asked them to imagine how their destiny might have changed had there been peep shows rather than churches on every corner. She brought them into remembrance of their own happy childhoods, growing up in towns where picnics were the big attraction. One by one the town council members cast their vote—"NO"—even though it meant surrendering needed tax revenue. They chose a different future, because they'd been brought into remembrance of a happier past.

In order to encourage people to accomplish something great, leaders must first bring them into remembrance—of successes past, of what was left behind, of the joys that lie ahead, of the reasons for changing. "With malice toward none . . . with charity toward all . . ." were words Abraham Lincoln used to help heal divisions in this country after the Civil War. He called the people to lay down their anger and remember what they all had in common—a love of God . . . and of their fellow man.

"It is my duty, as long as I am in this tent, to keep stirring you up with reminders." —2 Peter 1:13

Jesus brought them into remembrance.

Question

What obstacles are you encountering that might call for a moment of remembrance about why you began this journey in the first place?

Question

Who best brings you into remembrance?

Power Connection:

Dear Lord, when I face challenging situations, help me take a moment and remember all Your gifts and blessings and saving ways. Help me cause others to reflect on our heritage and history in You.

Amen.

I, _____ bring them into remembrance.

He Shaped the Invisible

Jesus did shape the invisible—with his faith. And he told us that was our gift and responsibility, as well. "If you ask for anything in my name, I will do it." —John 14:14. So often we emphasize the "Pray to get things" aspect of the power that it is diminished to the level of having our basic needs or desires met. But prayer and faith are actually *the shaping power of the future*.

I know many cases of parents who committed prayers to their passion and created the child they longed for. My friend Jan Sterrett recalls when her daughter Linda was born. Jan awoke still groggy from the anesthesia and was momentarily alone in her room. She suddenly saw an angel standing at the foot of her bed, who smiled and said, "You have a little girl, and she will have long, curly brown hair just as you requested." When they brought in the baby with a crop of curly brownish hair covering her crown, Jan wept with delight. She knew her prayers had helped shape the invisible.

Newsweek magazine recently reported, "Even quantum mechanics, the study of subatomic interactions, offers evidence that the world does not come into being until a mind interacts with it. Eminent physicist John Wheeler of Princeton University refers to us living in (an observer-) created universe. Bizarre though it seems, for instance, measuring the spin of one subatomic particle forces a twin particle miles away to have the opposite spin. The observer literally creates reality, much as Eastern and other holistic faiths teach." (*Newsweek*, November 28, 1994)

Research in quantum physics has discovered particles that take on properties proportionate to the expectations of the people watching them. Perhaps these are the creative particles hovering in the universe, which are merely awaiting our clear commands. "God said, 'Light, Be.' And Light was." — Genesis 1:3

When our founding fathers met in Philadelphia, they declared that their purpose was "to create a more perfect union." They then went on to describe what the core elements and rights would be in this more perfect union—such as the right to pursue life, liberty, and happiness. They went on to describe in detail the belief that in their union every citizen would have the right to bear arms and be guaranteed other freedoms such as freedom of the press and separation of church and state. The visionaries who met in a single room with their prayers and their pens shaped the invisible—creating the framework that supports what is considered the most successful form of government now known. They did not have a role model to look at as they wrote their words—they had only their faith and their imagination. These people truly *shaped the invisible*.

In the Book of Wisdom, we are told that "Wisdom makes choice of the works God is to do."—Wisdom 8:3–4. Clearly, we, too, are given the option to help direct the works of God.

When Jesus told the little girl to wake up, or Lazarus to come out of the tomb, or the cripple to rise up off of his pallet and walk, he was altering their future, viewing it not as a destiny carved in stone, but one filled with new possibility and hope. He was changing each person's previously perceived destiny.

Jesus shaped the invisible.

Question
What tools are you using to shape the invisible?

Question
What shape do you want your invisible future to have?

Power Connection:

Dear Lord, You and I can shape the invisible. Help me realize the ongoing creative power of my thoughts and words. Remind me that the future is not a train coming at me but rather a blank canvas placed before me. May I always shape the invisible into forms of truth and beauty.

Amen.

I, _____, shape the invisible.

He Knew That Success
Is Cumulative

I read recently that during a typical rainfall, a single acre of land will receive five million raindrops in one hour's time.

With this in mind, one comes to realize that no single raindrop carries more weight than any other. The first stroke in the pool is as significant as the final one that leads to the victory stand at the Olympics. Yet so many of us subconsciously believe that success will happen overnight . . . that we can start swimming one week and be an Olympic champion the next.

God knows that success is cumulative. Had Jesus not believed that his work would outlast him, he would have been in despair on the cross, considering himself at that point in time to be a failure. Instead, he was able to say, "It is finished." He knew that success was cumulative. *All* his deeds add up to success.

I love watching small drops of water on a windowpane

merge with others in that unique combination of chemistry and gravity that turns one drop of water into a rivulet, then a stream. In business and in life we must patiently take the steps that, combined, will lead to the success we crave. We must remember that success is not a destination, but a *process*. As long as we are engaged in the process(es) of what we want to be doing, we can consider ourselves a daily or even hourly success.

My sister Kathy had wanted a new house for fifteen years. As the wife of a farmer, however, she knew that the land's needs come first and decorating desires second. She finally settled on redecorating the old farmhouse they lived in, and decided to rejoice in the new carpet and furniture when it arrived. Though she did her best to make a silk purse out of a sow's ear, she continued to pray for her ideal. Then one hot summer's night, lightning hit a nearby power line, and the resulting surge of electricity set one of the children's rooms on fire. The family escaped, only to watch helplessly as their house burned to the ground before fire trucks from the distant city could arrive.

The next day Kathy, her husband Ben and the three children wandered through the ashes in shock. Now even the house they'd had was gone. And since it had been such an old structure, the insurance did not cover the replacement cost. To make things worse, the rain had destroyed the cotton crops, so there would be little or no money left to rebuild. They moved into another old house on the farm, which was worse than the former one, and began to regroup. Kathy, now in mourning, tried once again to beautify an old structure.

However, Ben knew that success was cumulative. He drew up a new house plan, based on Kathy's long expressed wishes. He gathered his farm workers, and from the mud, straw, and clay on the farm they began making adobe bricks—one by one. As money came in, they started construction on the new home, built on the foundation of the old one. When money was tight, they stopped. One season the floorboards were ruined because there hadn't been enough funds to put up the roof before the rains came. They had to be pulled up and completely replaced the next spring. Yet every day after hours Ben and his farm workers built, using the tools and resources they had.

Finally, *five years later*, Kathy, Ben, and the kids moved into their new six-thousand-square-foot adobe dream home. The cotton crops had been good for three consecutive years. Not only was the house paid for in cash, but every brick in it had been made by hand, shaped by her husband from the land she loved. Ben became my hero because not even fire and lightning had stopped him from finally completing my sister's dream.

"The kingdom of heaven is like a farmer."—Mark 4:3
Jesus knew that success is cumulative.

Question

Which efforts of yours will be cumulative?

Question

Where in your life or your work are you expecting instant success?

Question

What resources do you have that you can begin shaping by hand?

Power Connection:

Dear Lord, help me realize that it is the accumulated sum of my words and deeds that form my life. Help me know that no one raindrop alone can water a field of wheat.

Amen.

I, _____ , know that success is cumulative.

He Knew the Land of Ghosts Would Give Birth

Isaiah prophesied, "Your dead will come back to life. The land of ghosts will give birth." —Isaiah 26:19

Many of us have places in our mind that might be called "the land of ghosts." One doesn't live long in this world without encountering memories that haunt us—coming back again and again to create a feeling of sadness, uneasiness, or despair. Any of us can look into our past and find a valley of dead, dried out bones.

Nowhere is this more evident than in the story of Ezekiel 37:

The hand of Yahweh was on me; he carried me away by the spirit of Yahweh and set me down in the middle of the Valley, a Valley full of bones. He made me walk up and down and all around them. There were vast quantities of these bones on the floor of the Valley; and they were completely dry. He said to me, "Son of man, can these bones live?" I said, "You know, Lord." He said, "Prophesy over these bones. Say, Dry bones, hear the word of Yahweh. The Lord says this to the bones; I am now going to make breath enter you, and you will live. I shall put sinews on you. I shall make flesh grow on you. I shall cover you with skin and give you breath, and you will live, and you will know that I am Yahweh."

I prophesied as I had been ordered. While I was prophesying there was a noise, a clattering sound; it was the bones coming together. And as I looked, they were covered with sinews; flesh was growing on them and skin was covering them, yet there was no breath in them. He said to me, "Prophesy to the breath; prophesy, son of man. Say to the breath, The Lord Yahweh says this: Come from the four winds, breath; breathe on these dead, so that they come to life." I prophesied as he had ordered me, and the breath entered them; they came to life and stood up on their feet, a great, an immense army.

Ezekiel was literally seeing a land of ghosts give birth.

For some of us the valley of bones might be a relationship gone bad. For the athlete or businessperson it may be a missed field goal or a lost opportunity. It might be something as tragic as the sudden death of a loved one, or something as simple as a wrong road taken, which created a delay. It might be an unrealized dream or unfulfilled potential that haunts us.

A dear friend of mine is an incredibly gifted, award-winning artist who has chosen to teach school and raise two small boys. She said she felt only sadness when she visited art galleries, because the ghost of an art career that she fears may never be realized haunted her.

One day I invited her to a gallery showing of her former art teacher's works. She reluctantly accepted. After we had gone into the gallery, greeted her former teacher, viewed his latest pieces, and left, she sighed, "One more fear overcome." When I asked her what she meant by that she confessed, "One of my nightmares has been that I would run into Mike, and he would stare at me and ask me what I was doing artistically, and I would have to say, 'Nothing.' " "Well, did it happen?" I asked. "Exactly as I dreamed it," she said "When he asked me what I was doing artistically . . . I told him I was doing nothing." I watched her closely for any signs of sadness, but was surprised to see only relief on her face.

Three months have passed and she is now taking courses in computer graphics and design and has begun illustrations for a children's book. Her walk into "the land of ghosts" had given birth to a new enthusiasm and determination. "And the bones stood up, an exceedingly great army."

When Jesus told us that all tears would be wiped away, he was saying that tears can also give birth to joy.

Those pains and mistakes and failures that haunt us can give birth to their exact opposite. If we are willing to face them and walk through them, we will discover that all fears are really ghosts of false evidence appearing real.

Jesus said, "Kill me if you must. Bury me in a tomb. Leave me for dead. Gamble for my clothes. Try to wash your hands of any memory of me. You can tear down this temple stone by stone and in three days I will raise it up again."

He knew the land of ghosts would give birth.

Question

What ghosts or dry bones from your past are haunting you? Name them.

Question

What would the bones look like if God suddenly put flesh and muscle on them and caused them to breathe and live?

Question

Do you believe that these "dead" bones can live?

Question

Do you believe that the ghosts haunting you can, if faced properly, lead to a new birth?

Power Connection:

Dear Lord, free me from the ghosts of my past. Help me name them and face them, and walk through them—with You—into a land of joy. Help the dry bones in all my valleys of despair rise up into a well-muscled army—ready for Your command.

Amen.

I, _____, know my land of ghosts will give birth.

He Went on a Walkabout

The Australian Aborigines have a term for a journey that is part vacation, part education, part initiation, and part religious ceremony. It is called a walkabout. It is a "pattern interrupt" of major consequence.

In her book *Mutant Message Down Under*, author Marlo Morgan chronicles her experiences with a tribe of Australian Aborigines. Believing she had been invited to meet with their elders so that they could officially thank her for the work that she had done on behalf of poor Aboriginal youth, she was astounded when instead of handing her a plaque they asked her to forfeit her jewelry, burn her clothes, and head barefoot into the wilderness with them.

She emerged from her journey not only with tribal secrets but most important with an understanding of herself—and how harmonious relationships become a life-or-death matter out in the bush.

Her story is an allegory for a situation many of us are facing today. Believing that the company or spouse or job or cause we've served faithfully all these years is about to reward us, we may instead be confronted with a strange-faced, naked reality that tells us to forfeit our jewels, burn our former wardrobe, and head barefoot into the wilderness.

Jesus was asked by God to do exactly that. No more building tables and chairs. It's time to say good-bye to the comfort of your mother who adores you, and head out on a walkabout.

Walkabouts are amazing things. When you are stripped of your Day Timers and agendas you become open to, and aware of, many joys, truths, and discoveries that you had missed before.

It's said that a turning point in former president George Bush's unsuccessful bid for reelection was when he professed amazement at how groceries were now being checked and scanned in stores. It also didn't help that he didn't know the price of a gallon of milk. Had he taken a walkabout prior to the campaign, he might have been more in touch with the issues (and prices) that were becoming a concern to his constituency.

A walkabout is also a worthy means for regaining or restoring sanity.

Many Americans are far too driven. Despite all our technological advances, we work longer and harder than ever before. Perhaps we should start walking around more. Meet the neighbors. Pet the dogs. Notice which trees are budding, and when. We need to get out of our ruts and our channels and our molelike routines and look up–look out–get moving in an open-faced, empty-handed, barefooted sort of way. I love Robert Frost's poem, "The Pasture":

> I'm going out to clean the pasture spring;
> I'll only stop to rake the leaves away
> (And wait to watch the water clear, I may):
> I shan't be gone long.—You come too.

> I'm going out to fetch the little calf
> That's standing by the mother. It's so young,
> It totters when she licks it with her tongue.
> I shan't be gone long.—You come too.

Frost is entreating us to break our routines and see God's beauty just out in the pasture.

"As Jesus was walking beside the Sea of Galilee, he saw two brothers. . . Peter and Andrew. . . . Going on from there, he saw two other brothers, James and John. Jesus called them, and immediately they left their boat and father and followed him."—Matthew 4:18–21 Jesus called out, "Drop your nets and follow me!"

He went on a walkabout.

Question

Describe your routine. Whom do you see? Where do you go for lunch? What are you usually doing on Monday, Wednesday, Friday, Saturday, and Sundays?

Question

What "mental" walkabout could you begin to get you out of your routine?

Question

Plan a walkabout for yourself that includes only a location and time frame, but no appointments. Make it someplace you have never gone before.

Question

Could you, would you drop your nets to follow God on an "unplanned" journey?

Power Connection:

Dear Lord, help me loosen up, shed my current costume, and head out with You on a walkabout. Let me not prejudge or label anything I see or try to predict the outcomes. Let me, too, lay my hammer down and walk with You to a land that shimmers in the distance, just beyond my sight.

Amen.

I, _____, go on a walkabout.

He Saw Himself as the Host

When Jesus turned water into wine at the wedding feast at Cana, an event at which he was a *guest*, he actually took on the duties of the *host*. This deed, I believe, eloquently conveyed his attitude toward the world. "He came not to be served, but to serve."—John 2:1

When I started my business, I began the task of networking as if the life of the company depended on it. In fact, it did because I had no money for advertising. The only way I could let people know about the service I provided was to show up in person and tell them. A colleague gave me very wise advice about how to take the discomfort out of the many networking parties I attended. She said, "Act as if you're the host at the party, rather than the guest."

I tried it both ways. I went to one party and acted like the guest (since that was the much easier assignment). I waited for someone to come up to me and ask me who I was and whether I had enough to eat and whether the tempera-ture of the room was okay with me and if the music was too loud, etc. That night I met two people.

The next week I took the other approach. I pretended that the party was actually my own and made sure to reach out to people who looked a little nervous and do what I could to introduce them to others (even though I knew no one there myself). The results were astoundingly different. I came home with twenty business cards from people whom I had actually connected with—because I had treated them as my guests. Acting like the host led me to reach out to more people. It put me in a proactive, rather than a reactive, stance.

My niece Tara (who was born a redhead) doesn't have a shy bone in her body. When my sister took her to school for the first time she told her, "Tara, try to make at least one new friend today." When Kathy picked her up that after-noon, Tara practically leaped into the car. "I made six friends today, Mommy!" she smiled. When Kathy asked her how she had done that, the six-year-old answered, "Well, I just looked around the playground at all the kids and said to my-self, "I'll just pretend that this is my birthday party, and 'Let 'er rip!' "

I recently stayed at the Philadelphia Airport Marriot. Being a frequent traveler, I am used to varying degrees of ser-vice. What impressed me about this place was how courte-ous and friendly everyone was to me—from the clerk at the check-in desk to the bellman who helped me with my luggage to the person who delivered room service to the person who took my messages. Finally, as I was leaving, I turned to the shuttle driver and said, "Why do I feel so cared about here? This place has been wonderful." He smiled and said, "Well, Ms. Jones, the way I see it, when you're here, you are my guest, and I want to do everything in my power to make sure you feel like this is your second home. I guess everyone else who works here feels the same way."

In the book *The Aladdin Factor*, authors Jack Canfield and Mark Victor Hanson have developed a formula to use as an aid for extending yourself. They use the initials SWSWSWSW, which stands for "Some Will, Some Won't, So What, Someone's Waiting." This acronym is an excellent encouragement for putting yourself out to others in new and perhaps challenging ways. Some will receive you. Some won't. So what? Someone's waiting.

Jesus knew that not everybody would want to come to his party. Nevertheless, he was concerned about the ones who would accept his invitation. He wasn't there to be invited—he was there to invite.

He saw himself as the host.

Question

Experiment with each of these two attitudes the next time you encounter someone new.

1. You are their guest.
2. You are their host.

Question
    Which is more comfortable?

Question
    Which yielded more pleasing results?

Question
    If this life isn't your party, whose party is it?

Power Connection:
    Dear Lord, help me act as the host eager to embrace others, not the guest, waiting to be served. Help me realize that joy in life is in serving others, not in being served. Grant me Your spirit of friendliness and generosity and hospitality.
    Amen.

I, _____, act as the host, not the guest.

He Had Eyes to See

After my brother Joe had a radial keratotomy to correct his vision, he was so enthusiastic about the results that he recruited several of his friends to also have the procedure. Having worn glasses or contacts for nearly twenty-five years, he found that suddenly being able to see without having to scramble for his lenses was something so amazing that he spoke about it with evangelical zeal.

Joe's experience made me think about the blind man Jesus healed. How precious must have been those first few moments of sight, when darkness gave way to light, distinct forms emerged from shadows, and then colors and shapes burst forth. Annie Dillard shares in her book *Pilgrim at Tinker Creek* that surgeons who work to restore sight to people who have been blind all their lives are careful to note that sudden new sight requires a psychological as well as a physiological adjustment. Some patients could see only for a few hours at a time before asking to have their eyes shaded or closed by masks so they could rest. The sudden influx of visual stimuli is a shock to their systems.

Jesus dealt with the issue of sightedness in many ways. He called the scribes and Pharisees "blind guides." He told them that because they claimed to see, but chose not to, their sin would remain.

Doesn't everybody have eyes? Doesn't everybody see? Apparently not. My brother's experience made me want to have an operation so that I, too, could get "a new pair of eyes." Not with sight that measures 20/20, but with a vision that can see people and issues the way God does.

Georgia O'Keeffe said, "To see a flower takes time, just like to have a friend takes time." Sight is an innate gift, but true vision must be trained. That's what Jesus meant when he said, "You have eyes, yet still do not see!" —Mark 8:18

I envy artists' eyes, because they have learned to look for details in form and texture and shadings. Their eyes realize that shadows are not made of the color gray, but are actually composed of blue and green and purple.

My mother can look at a face and sketch it almost perfectly, because she has eyes that were trained to see. During the Depression she used to earn lunch money by doing sketches of movies stars and selling them for a nickel. She once told me that she especially enjoyed doing the Dionne quintuplets. I calculated quickly and said, "Mom, that amounted to a penny a face!" "Come to think of it, you're right!" she laughed, "but drawing babies is so much fun." I know that whenever we meet someone, she is seeing him or her differently than I am. She is noticing the length of his nose or where her eyebrows meet or the shape of his lips and the color tones of her skin and the relationship of the eyelids to the cheekbone. I look at the person and think, *Oh, how nice* and then try to remember his or her name. Going on a walk with my mother can often take hours because she has to stop at each flower and study and absorb and reflect on its colors. "To see a flower takes time . . ."

I recently stood in amazement at the El Prado museum in Madrid, looking at a painting of Saint Bartholomew by Rubens. Rubens had captured the blue veins in the man's hand and the way the light came through the tip of his ear and turned it orange. It was this little burst of orange on an otherwise dark painting that made the whole work come alive. A magnificent work by Velázquez portrayed a soldier on a horse, with the breeze billowing in the horse's mane. Its tail was swirling in symphonic harmony with the flag the soldier carried. Who else in life would see that the motion in the flag and the mane and the tail of a horse was all one movement? Only those with eyes that see.

What if each of us could take training to see into the human heart? What if we could view situations before us rightly—with the eyes of God. "She isn't dead, she's sleeping," Jesus said of the little girl before him. —Matthew 9:24

He saw the situation differently from all of those around him, and his vision proved to be true. "Sculpture may be almost anything: a monument, a statue, an old coin, a bas-relief, a portrait bust, a lifelong struggle against heavy odds."—Malvina Hoffman, *Sculpture Inside and Out* (1939)

Jesus observed people putting their money into the treasury one day. Many rich people threw in large amounts, while a poor widow put in only a fraction of a penny. Calling his disciples to him, Jesus said "This poor widow has put more into the treasury than all the others, for they gave out of their wealth, but she put in all she had."—Mark 12:41–43

Jesus had eyes that see.

Question

Do you look at situations with only two eyes?

Question

When have you not seen a situation clearly, and later found out how blind you were? What could have prevented your blindness?

Question

How can people have eyes and yet not see clearly?

What can you do—what are you doing—to correct your vision?

What situation do you wish you could see more clearly?

Describe in detail how Christ probably sees it.

Power Connection:

Dear Lord, I look at the world through a dark and dim glass. I see only in one or two dimensions sometimes—filtering my perceptions through my very limited focus and prejudices. Open my eyes. Open my heart. Open my mind. Give me eyes that truly see.

Amen.

I, _____ , have eyes to see.

He Went to the
Answering Place

Many of us are wandering through life with questions, not realizing there is an answering place. When Jesus was wrestling with the question of his upcoming crucifixion, he went into the garden to pray. He went to the answering place.

Grace Cathedral in San Francisco has a labyrinth that is designed as a meditation place. A person stands quietly in the beginning of the circle and proceeds to the first point. There she is asked to present her concerns. Then she advances to the next turning point, and is asked to shed her resentments. This labyrinth continues with a gradual shedding of fears, asking for courage, shedding of anger, and asking for reconciliation, until at the end of the walk the person is said to emerge more clear about her direction. The Reverend Dr. Lauren Artress, canon at Grace Cathedral, has now devoted herself full-time to a ministry that encourages the construction of labyrinths in public places around the world. Because the labyrinth is devoted solely to meditation and reflection, it is "an answering place."

"As your word unfolds, it gives light," wrote David in Psalm 119:130. David often went up into the hills, "from whence his help came." He went to his answering place.

Moses went into the hills to receive his instructions from God. He often "talked to God face to face," and asked him many questions. When he was given specifications on how to construct the temple, he was told, "See that you make all these things according to the pattern that you saw on the mountain." —Exodus 25:40. It was in the answering place that Moses received his directions.

Many stories have been documented in Scripture and history of people setting out on a journey presuming to know the answers. In an amazing tale documented in Numbers 14, the Israelites who had listened to spies trying to incite a rebellion against Moses had a sudden change of heart (after the spies were struck dead before them). "They were up early the next morning, and started towards the Promised Land. 'Here we are!' they said. 'We realize that we have sinned, but now we are ready to go on into the land the Lord has promised us.' Moses warned them not to go. 'Now you are disobeying the Lord's orders to return to the wilderness. Don't go ahead with your plan or you will be crushed by your enemies, for the Lord is not with you!' But they went ahead presumptuously, even though the ark of the covenant did not go with them. Then the Amalekites and the Canaanites who lived in the hills came down and attacked them and chased them back to Horman." —Numbers 14:40–45 (*The Living Bible*). These people failed because they had not gone to the answering place. They acted presumptuously on the information they thought they had and were defeated because of it.

Many of us act on information without having carefully pondering it. "Zeal is not good where reflection is wanting. He who goes too quickly misses his way." —Proverbs 19:2. All of us need to take time apart and get quiet, and listen for answers as we make decisions that affect the lives of others.

One year I served as Executive Director for the YWCA Girl's Camp. There was a place behind the cabins called Inspiration Point where we held our Sunday services and the staff would go each day to watch the sunset. The point had a magnificent view that overlooked the valley below. One day one of the girls who had been among the most challenging asked me to walk with her up the mountain. I did, and about two-thirds of the way up the path, she stepped off the trail and asked me to look down. There, a few yards off the path, was a small area that had been cleared of all the weeds and brush and was surrounded by a circle of carefully placed rocks. "I cleared away everything but the wildflowers." She smiled self-consciously as I surveyed this gift. "From here you can see all of us down below," she said, pointing to the view, which took in the recreation field and each of the cabins. "That is why I picked this spot." She paused and then said softly, her eyes looking at the ground, "I know I've been a lot of trouble for you, and some of the other girls have, too, and I thought this might be a good place for you to come and get some answers," she said. "That is beautiful, Carol," I said. "I will call this 'The Answering Place.'" Many times I went there, especially after the camp had ended and all I had for company was the echo of the kids laughing and shouting in the hills.

I realize, now more than ever, I need to go back to "The Answering Place." I need a viewpoint that allows me to look down on the everyday happenings of my life and see them as God sees them, placed in their proper perspective. Our world seems to be traveling faster and faster as it gets smaller and smaller, and we need answers now more than ever. Yet I find it a sad commentary that in many hospitals the chapel has been converted into a physical therapy room. In San Diego a once beautiful church called The Abbey is now a nightclub. Is it any wonder that as we "pave paradise to put in a parking lot" we are consuming more mood-elevating and mind-altering drugs than any nation in the world? Perhaps it is because we have stopped building and nurturing and seeking the answering places.

"Jesus went into the garden to pray."—Matthew 26:36
He went to The Answering Place.

Question

Where in your life are you acting on "information" without seeking "answers"?

Question

Why would it be wise to shed your resentments before seeking answers?

Question

Where is your answering place, and how often do you go there?

Question

Where in society could we build, nurture, or create more "answering places"?

Power Connection:

Dear Lord, please remind me to go to the answering place before I head out on my journey. Help me be still. Help me listen. Help me understand that You are in the business of building souls, a work that exceeds human understanding. Help me rest in the quiet confidence of You.

Amen.

I, _____, go to the answering place.

Passion

passion: (pash'en) *n.* **1.** compelling emotion **2.** strong amorous feeling; love **3.** strong sexual desire, lust **4.** a strong fondness, enthusiasm, or desire for something **5.** the object of one's passion **6.** an outburst of emotion **7.** violent anger; wrath; rage **8.** the sufferings of Christ on the cross or subsequent to the Last Supper.

(Random House Webster's College Dictionary)

Every person you see around you is the result of a passionate encounter, as are you and I. Passion is the force that ensures the creation of new life. It is the essence of creativity, the heart of strong desire. I find it interesting that the *Webster's Collegiate Dictionary* defines passion as being sexual desire as well as the feelings of Christ. Jesus demonstrated God's passionate desire toward us. He described himself as a bridegroom seeking his bride. He urged that we might be "one," using the same term as the "two becoming one flesh" described in the marriage ceremony. He poured his life out in passionate, meaningful encounters with everyone he met. He held nothing back.

When Jesus called out to the fishermen to leave their nets, he was appealing to their passion to live a meaningful life. When he told the woman at the well that what she really wanted was living water, she dropped her bucket, splashing lesser water all over her, and ran to get her friends.

Jesus calls us to passion-filled lives.

"I have come to bring *fire*." —Luke 12:49

He Thrust His Hand through the Door

The image of Jesus standing patiently at the door and knocking is familiar to many of us. But lately I've been reading and rereading the Song of Solomon, and a verse in it keeps resounding in my head.

> My Beloved thrust his hand
> through the hole in the door
> and I trembled to the core of my being.
> —SONG OF SOLOMON 5:4

He didn't just tap on the door, ring the doorbell, or jiggle the lock: The Beloved put a hole in the door trying to get to the one he loved!

When a sudden, unexpected change occurs in your life, God may be thrusting his hand through your door. Jesus had a passion that grabbed people by the heart and turned all their ideas and prejudices upside down. He startled them into the recognition that there was more to life than just lying around on their pallets. He took the initiative to reach inside their comfort zone and wake them up. He thrust his hand through the door.

Firemen carry axes with them, as well as water hoses. They know all too well that they may have to burst through a wall, or knock down a door in order to save the life inside.

Gideon was hiding in a wine vat until an angel "whooshed" down and thrust his hand through the door. "Come out, Gideon. We need you." —Judges 6:12

Nehemiah was happily serving wine to a king until a message of his Jewish brethren's despair thrust God's hand through his door. —Nehemiah 1

Simon was contentedly casting out his net until he heard a voice calling out, "Follow me!" —Mark 1:17. And suddenly God's hand thrust through the door.

People who, like the apostle Paul, have been knocked off their feet by a cataclysmic change in plans, are experiencing God's hand bursting through the door. When we experience an illness or a sudden change in plans, we also are feeling God's hand thrusting through our door.

Yet how do we apply that to our own approach to life? How do we thrust our hand through another's door?

There are numerous ways to do so. I feel the finest way

is to call the question—to go directly to the heart of a situation and speak the truth about it. I have had the seemingly harsh words of others pierce my soul and send me into a time of needed reevaluation. As I recounted in *The Path*, my boss and mentor, Catherine Calhoun, thrust her hand through my door when she said, "Why are you trying to be a social worker? That isn't your highest gift!"

I've thrust my hand through the doors of others, challenging one friend to face the truth about an unhappy marriage, suggesting to another that he was in the wrong job.

We can and must thrust our hand through the door if we see someone caught in a downward spiral or about to injure him or herself. The friends who put a hole in the roof of the house where Jesus was speaking, so they could lower down their paralyzed friend, were demonstrating a passionate desire to see a life take a different direction.—Mark 2:4

Robert Muëller, former assistant Secretary General to the United Nations, says "Death is not the tragedy. The tragedy is what we let die while we live."

Jesus thrust his hand through the door.

Question

Are you just politely ringing doorbells when there is something or someone vitally important dying on the other side?

Question

　　When has someone thrust a hand through *your* door?

Question

　　When have you experienced a sudden encounter with
God that caused you to tremble to the core of your being?

Power Connection:

　　Dear Lord, help me to be open to a mission, a message,
a passion so strong that I am willing to thrust my hand
through the door to reach it. Cause me to tremble to the core
of my being with Your power, Your presence, and Your love.
　　Amen.

I, _____, thrust my hand through
the door.

He Had Thunder in His Hooves

A friend who had not seen me for many years bought me a magnificent copper and silver horse pin for my birthday. As she carefully pinned it onto my sweater she said, "You must be sure to wear this right over your heart." When I asked her why, she paused, looked at me, and replied, "Because it is the beating of your heart that gives it the thunder in its hooves."

It was the beating of God's heart that gave Jesus the thunder in his hooves. He had an intimate connection to the Passion that not only sets the world in motion, but also steers it on its course; who not only breathes life into the human body, but also yearns to see its spirit totally expressed. Jesus said, "My very nourishment comes from doing the will of God who sent me, and for finishing his work." —John 4:34. These words reflected a longing that came from deep within—a calling that was not a mere job description, but the mission flowing in his veins. "Before I knew it, my passion had hurled me onto the chariots of my people, as their prince." —Song of Solomon 6:12

Some historians state that civilization began when man discovered how to harness fire. The point could be made that we have done perhaps too good a job at harnessing it and not a very good job of stirring up the fire that is within us.

These days Hollywood has a plethora of movies that have little plot yet lots of explosives. It seems when the writers or directors run out of dialogue they decide to blow up a building, a body, or a car. These explosions often belie the lack of passion in the movie's message. There are fireworks for the eyes, but no dynamite for the heart.

Despite all our external successes, the United States is statistically the most depressed, suicidal, voluntarily sedated and drugged nation in the world. Millions of us have not found the beating in our hearts. Where is our passion?

What is it you would do even if you weren't paid to do so? What are you involved in that throws you into a state of absolute concentration and timelessness?

The world watched in awe as Michael Johnson stepped into the runners' blocks in anticipation of the 400-meter race that would catapult him into history. When the gun sounded his golden shoes ran faster than any man has ever run before. Any of us who watched the event knew he wanted to win and that what carried him was the thunder in his feet.

In the book of Job reference is made to the war horse that "scents the battle from afar":

> *Exultantly he paws the soil of the valley,*
> *and prances eagerly to meet the clash of arms.*
> *He laughs at fear; he is afraid of nothing,*
> *he recoils before no sword.*
> *Quivering with impatience, he eats up the miles;*
> *when the trumpet sounds, there is no holding him.*
> *At each trumpet blast he shouts "Hurrah!"*
> *He scents the battle from afar,*
> *hearing the thundering of chiefs,*
> *the shouting.*
>
> —JOB 39:21–25

We, too, need to paw the dirt in front of us, eager to engage the clashes in the valleys. We need to feel the thunder in our hooves.

The same passion that drove Jesus to overturn tables in the temple compelled him to turn toward Jerusalem. When the trumpet sounded, there was no holding him.

He had thunder in his hooves.

Question

Do you have thunder in your hooves, or lead?

Question

What mission would excite you enough to become like a war horse, eager for the scent of battle?

Question

What mission in your life has you "quivering with impatience, eating up the miles"?

Power Connection:

Dear Lord, rekindle in me Your sense of urgency, excitement, and power. Let me be like the war horse, pawing the field, eager to engage in Your holy work. Fill me with the divine impatience Jesus had. Give me the courage of the horse that laughs at fear, recoils before no sword, and trembles at nothing.

Amen.

I, _____, have thunder in my hooves.

He Practiced
His Highest Gift

Jesus was probably a very good carpenter. Fortunately for us, he chose instead to practice his *highest* gift. I am always fascinated to learn about the earlier careers of famous people. I can't help but wonder when they had an inkling that what they were currently doing was not their ultimate destiny. Gary Larson, one of the world's funniest cartoonists, spent his early days as a dog catcher. My friends and I used to enjoy going to a place in San Diego called The Littlest Kitchen where the famous actress Whoopi Goldberg was once a dishwasher. A young man named Mike, who used to seem quite content painting houses and drinking beer on the weekends, is now enrolled in medical school. At what point, exactly, did he get it in his head that maybe painting houses wasn't his highest gift? At what point do any of us get it? And, sadly, how many of us never do?

Sometimes we don't practice our highest gifts because we

don't know what they are. Chances are, if something comes gracefully and naturally and easily to you, it is probably a gift. Nurture and encourage it and make room for it in your life. "Follow your heart" is always good advice when it comes to discovering your highest gift.

My father wanted me to be a professional tennis player. Believe me, that was not my highest gift. Yet his desire for me to succeed in the sport was so intense that when I told him I had dropped varsity tennis in order to accommodate my journalism classes, he quit speaking to me for several very pain-filled days. Family members often place unwitting limitations, boundaries, obstacles, or pressures on us that keep us from practicing our highest gifts.

"In the course of their journey he came to a village, and a woman named Martha welcomed him into her house. She had a sister named Mary, who sat down at the Lord's feet and listened to him speak. Now Martha who was distracted with all the serving said, 'Lord, do you not care that my sister is leaving me to do the serving all by myself? Please tell her to help me.' But the Lord answers, 'Martha, Martha,' he said, 'you worry and fret about so many things, and yet few are needed, indeed only one. It is Mary who has chosen the better part; it is not to be taken from her.' " —Luke 10:42 (*New Jerusalem Bible*)

In this case Mary chose to practice her *highest* gift— which was not doing the dishes but listening to the Lord. She was the one, remember, who later recognized his voice in the garden and thus became the first evangelist.

In the wilderness Jesus had to ask himself, "What did I come here to do?" I believe each of us should ask ourselves that question. "Am I right now, in my work, career, or chosen activities, practicing my highest gift?" We get out of balance when we are *not* using our highest gifts.

Can you imagine what this world would be like if everyone who had the gift of music, sang . . . if all artists were truly free to paint . . . if dancers were encouraged to dance, rather than take a desk job? Why do people so often resemble racehorses pulling plows or tigers thinking they have to act like sheep? Surely it must be because we have enslaved ourselves—at some level—to a lesser god.

Jesus came to tell us to quit serving lesser gods and practice our highest gifts. "Don't you know I must be about my Father's business?" —Luke 2:49. He knew he would have to leave the carpentry shop.

He practiced his highest gift.

Question

What is your highest gift? Are you practicing it?

Question

Are you allowing and encouraging others to practice theirs?

Question

If you are not, who or what is the lesser god you are serving?

Power Connection:

Dear Lord, You have given each of us gifts to use for the
good of all. Help me claim and recognize my highest gift and
practice it—refusing to enslave my energies to a lesser god.
Help me encourage others to practice their highest gifts as
well, that Your kingdom may be multiplied and may abound.
Amen.

I, _____, practice my highest gift.

He Made It Memorable

One autumn I decided to take my friend Linda on a tour of the Napa Valley. She drove down from Portland and I drove up from San Diego, and we met in San Francisco. Wanting to show off my navigational skills, I insisted that she follow me on the route to Napa that I had carefully mapped out the night before. As rain and traffic engulfed us, I confidently honked and guided her onto the Bay Bridge. Unfortunately, this put us into Oakland during rush hour. I also had completely missed the turnoff for the Golden Gate Bridge, which was the correct route. Three and a half hours later—hours filled with freeway construction and countless stops and starts—we arrived at our destination. (Had I led her correctly, it would have been a forty-five-minute drive.) As we parked she very slowly got out of her car and walked up to mine. Since Linda is known for having—shall we say, volume—in her voice, I thought, *She is going to yell*. She opened the door, got into the passenger seat, and looked at me silently for a very long moment. Then she said, "Laurie, I have learned that when I am with you one thing is certain. Even the smallest event will be made *memorable*." And then she laughed and hugged me.

It is said that memory is the only paradise from which we cannot be driven. I believe that is why Jesus wanted to make events memorable. Some people theorize that he used the miracles only to get people's attention, so that as they gathered they would hear the real message—the one based not on healing the flesh but rather on healing the spirit. He knew that for the human mind to latch on to something, it has to witness something out of the ordinary.

When designer Siegfried Widmar and I ran an advertising agency together in La Jolla, I was amazed at how he could make everyday events memorable. When we had a client coming to visit, Siegfried would go to the nearby deli and get two special little gourmet chocolates. Then he would create a simple, elegant paper sculpture of a dove and write the client's name on it. Everyone who came to our office left with a sculpted dove and two chocolates. To this day clients tell me that they still have that dove in their offices. The entire effort took him maybe fifteen minutes of preparation. Yet, he made the visit memorable.

I'll never forget the waiter in Rome who put Parmesan

cheese on each guest's lasagna by lifting the plates over his head and then tossing the cheese fragments high in the air—catching the cheese at the last moment. I saw a lot of grated cheese in Italy, but this waiter made even that familiar event (and the restaurant) memorable.

A friend of mine was contemplating marriage to a man she had been dating steadily for three years. For some reason she just could not seem to make the "M" commitment. The two of them even went into therapy, both as a couple and as individuals to see what was holding her back. Finally, she decided against the marriage. When I asked her what was the key factor in her decision, she said, "I played out what it would be like to be with him in two years, five years, ten years from now. And you know what? I could predict it, right down to his golf schedule on Saturdays. That's when I knew I had to find someone else." This man lost her because he failed to make life memorable.

Each of us need to take the time to examine how we could make the ordinary *extra*ordinary. Maybe it's as simple as putting little love notes into a child's lunch box. Maybe it means hiring mariachis to sing a birthday sonata under a balcony. Chefs take simple food items and arrange them on plates so that they become works of art. Every event is capable of being made memorable. My friend Catherine used to exclaim as we were getting in the car, "Just think! We can go to lunch anywhere we want to in this whole city!" Or she'd say, "Look at us—driving back from the bank after being turned down for your first loan. This is a moment to be remembered!" She has a way of framing a thing—or an event—to make it memorable.

Jesus knew on the evening of Passover that it would be his last night on earth before returning to his Father. "So he got up from the supper table, took off his robe, wrapped a towel around his loins, poured water into a basin, and began to wash the disciples' feet. "You don't understand why I am doing this? Someday, you will." —John 13:7

He made it memorable.

Question

What did you create today that was memorable?

Question

What positive, memorable occasions have others created for you?

Power Connection:

Dear Lord, help me use my imagination and creativity to make everyday events more memorable. Give me the tiny extra spark, the extra ten minutes, to turn an ordinary event into a beautiful or delightful memory for others, knowing memory is the paradise from which we cannot be driven.

Amen.

I, _____, make it memorable.

He Described His Thirst

Jesus said, "I thirst." —John 19:28. He didn't just think it, imply it through his actions, or hope they would figure it out on their own. He accurately verbalized what he was feeling in the moment and expressed it out loud.

We need to learn how to describe our feelings accurately in order to communicate clearly with others. None of us is a mindreader. Although a two-year-old can communicate pretty clearly what he or she wants, as we age, we start burying our emotions or coloring them over.

I was recently in a convenience store with a friend who quietly pointed to a man at the counter. "See that man?" she whispered. "He's the one who ran over a cat in my neighborhood and then just drove off." "Are you going to say anything to him?" I asked her. "No," she whispered, "I'm just going to give him a dirty look." Which she did. That man had no more idea what her "look" was about than if she'd sent him a note written in Swahili. When you feel something, describe it—out loud and accurately.

"I am thirsting for a time when all people will be free," thundered the voice of Martin Luther King as he marched across the South. "We are thirsting for the right to govern our own land," wrote the founding fathers gathered in a smoky, candle-lit room in Philadelphia. "I am thirsting for a planet where there will be perpetual spring," wrote Rachel Carson, author of *Silent Spring,* and early leader of the environmental movement. Individuals who accurately describe their thirst attract people who are willing to help them quench it. "Follow me, and you will never be thirsty again," Jesus said, knowing that the woman at the well was thirsty for a new way of living, not just well water.

As confident as I am about writing feelings on paper I have been less successful in communicating my needs in person. I am working now on more accurately describing my thirst—*when* I feel it, and not two years later as I walk out the door. ("Oh, yeah, and by the way—I was really thirsty back then.") Clear and constant communication about our vulnerabilities is one way to keep connected with people. The fact that Jesus said "I thirst" with his dying breath was one more effort to let us into his world as he was leaving ours.

He described his thirst.

Question

How are you describing your thirst to others? Through direct, or indirect, communication?

Question

How could describing your thirst work to your advantage in negotiating with others?

Question

Who is currently trying to tell you about his or her thirst?

Power Connection:

Dear Lord, I thirst. I have needs and wants. Help me describe them in such a way that others hear and understand me—thus beginning an important circle of communication.

Amen.

I, _____, describe my thirst.

He Was a Fragrance Poured Out

"Your name is an oil poured out. How right it is to love you," begins the Song of Solomon, a book that is rich with imagery about the power of fragrance. In it the atmosphere around the Lover is described as "a column of smoke, breathing of myrrh and frankincense and every perfume the merchant knows."—Song of Solomon 3:6

After reading the Song a short time ago, I began to wonder how a person's name could be "a fragrance poured out." The most famous display of love for Jesus in the gospels was Mary's pouring fragrant anointing oil over Jesus' feet. People who claim to have had modern-day visions of Mary, the mother of Jesus, commonly report the fragrance of roses in the vicinity of where she appears. The scribe in Ecclesiasticus exhorts the people to "Blossom like the rose . . . and give off a sweet smell of incense . . . spread your fragrance abroad."—Ecclesiasticus 39:13–14 (*New Jerusalem Bible*)

Years ago, shortly after my father died, a friend asked me if I missed him. I surprised both the friend and myself by saying, "Well, actually I almost feel closer to him. While he was alive, he was just in his body. Now that the vessel has been destroyed, it's like he is a fragrance everywhere." It is not uncommon for people who are grieving to hold their precious one's clothes up to their face and breathe deeply, deeply, trying to capture the essence of their unique smell before it disappears. The laws of attraction in the animal kingdom are based largely on scent. Cosmetic companies make fortunes trying to convince us that they have the love potion that will attract our perfect lover.

I recently learned that while all other senses have a circuitous, filtered pathway to the brain, scent goes *directly* to a spot that automatically triggers all of the other senses, especially memory.

How can a person give off a fragrance? Is it reputation? Is it the glow of a feeling people have in that person's presence—a glow that lingers even after he or she is gone? Is it intention that is released into the air—invisible but traceable by those with nostrils to detect it? I have encountered people at airports or social gatherings whose memory lingered with me for days. Something about them gave off a fragrance that remained.

On a tour of a perfume factory in Nice, France, I learned that it takes one *ton* of rose petals to make an *ounce* of perfume. Surely it is the accumulated deeds and conversations and memories of a person that turn into the fragrance they leave behind.

Many Eastern traditions emphasize aroma as part of the healing process. I think we need more aromatherapy in our own lives. We should be able to sense the subtle odors of love when it is approaching or has just gone by. True love and passion are not demonstrated or measured in tangible, visible deeds alone. We must realize that our thoughts, words, and deeds become a fragrance that surrounds us. Love leaves a scent so subtle, yet so strong, that even a fawn could find it and follow it in a forest.

A new client of mine was concerned about letting his information and technology firm be a vehicle for communicating God's love in the world. As we discussed the many ways of doing so, he finally said, "I don't want to leave just a brochure in their office when I go. I want to leave behind the scent of God."

Jesus was a fragrance poured out.

Question

What fragrance do you pour out?

Question

If your friends and associates were to name *you* as a personal fragrance, what would it be? _____
- Worries of the world
- Optimism

- Doom and gloom
- Possibilities
- Other: _____

Power Connection:

Dear Lord, help me to be a fragrance poured out. Help me realize that the essence of my thoughts and deeds turn into subtle odors that can attract and delight others.

Amen.

I, _____, am a fragrance poured out.

He Shared His Life Force

I've often wondered why Jesus would curse a fig tree. It seemed so out of character for him to curse anything— much less a tree. If he was really hungry for a fig, he certainly knew how to create one. But in thinking about it, I have concluded that he cursed that tree because somehow, somewhere, it had consciously decided to withhold its own life force. How can God work with a being that has consciously and defiantly decided not to grow?

We have all probably met those who are so determined not to be taken that they refuse to give.

I once stood in line for twenty-five minutes at the county courthouse to file a document, only to be sent to another part of the building to obtain an additional form *after* I had finally reached the front of the line. When I asked the woman why they didn't have all the necessary forms in the same place, she replied dully, "I don't know. That's not my department.

Next!" I knew then how Jesus must have felt when he loosed some words at that tree. This woman was consciously withholding her life force from her customers, her coworkers, and herself. Haven't you met people like that—who were so intent on not being taken advantage of that they will not give?

A passage in the book of Wisdom reads: "To live—that is why the Creator made things." It also reads: "You love all that exists. You hold nothing of what you have made in abhorrence—for had You hated anything, you would not have formed it. And how, had You not willed it, could a thing persist—how be conserved if not called forth by You? You spare all things because all things are Yours, Lord, Lover of Life— You whose imperishable spirit is in all." —Wisdom 11:23 (*New Jerusalem Bible*)

In Ezekiel 47, the prophet paints a beautiful picture of a stream that begins as a mere trickle in the temple and then expands into a river too wide to swim across. "Everything will live where the river goes. There will be trees of many different kinds. And their fruit will be for food, their leaves for healing."—Ezekiel 47: 8–12. This is also an image that describes what occurs when people share their life force: their deeds create an ever-expanding river, teeming with life and possibilities.

Jesus said, "I am the vine." —John 15:1. He intended to bear fruit for others to enjoy.

He shared his life force.

Question

Where are you withholding your life force—at work, at home? Why?

Question

How are you *sharing* your life force?

Question

How do you feel when others
• share their life force with you?
• withhold their life force from you?

Power Connection:

Dear Lord, You have given me a life force to be poured out. Help me share my ideas, energies, and enthusiasm freely, just as You did.

Amen.

I, _____, share my life force.

He Kept His Altar Clean

All of us worship at an altar. It may not be visible, and it may not actually be in church, but without exception, each of us is worshipping at some version of an altar, because worshiping something is human nature. Wherever we are giving our utmost attention, our greatest gift of time and energy—there will our altar be. And for many of us, that altar is a cluttered one, piled high with big and little priorities that we shift from place to place, worshipping each one with our attention and devotion as needed.

When in a fury Jesus overturned the moneychangers' tables in the temple, his anger was not directed at business per se. Rather, he knew that the temple's altar had to be kept clean for its *true* business, which is prayer. "My father's house is a house of prayer," he said, "but you have made it a den of thieves!"—Matthew 21:13

Many people tried to clutter Jesus' altar. Satan himself

offered to put various and sundry items on it, such as bread, human adulation, and the keys to the world. Although it was a combination that would be attractive to almost anyone, Jesus swept each item off the altar and kept it clean.

A friend of mine who is a Lutheran minister was telling me about a class she took at Berkeley regarding social trends and mainstream denominationalism. She said that some recent studies show that the churches that are growing at breakneck speed are the ones that: (1) offer a lot of entertainment, or (2) practice walling off their congregations from the world, claiming to be the only safe and holy place. Hollywood or Armageddon. Nice choices. It made me wonder what is really on the altars of those churches, and what is on the altars of the people they're attracting?

But more important, what is on mine? What do I worship with my time and talents? Which god am I *really* serving when I head out into my day? When I come home at night, what new gods do I dump on the altar, as if emptying my pockets or shopping bags? It takes a daily, diligent effort for me to simply keep my dining room table clean. Because it is right by the entrance to my home, I tend to unload everything I've carried from the car onto it. My altar is like that dining room table, requiring daily maintenance to keep it free of clutter.

It is easy to pick up the gods of the culture we live in. Recall that the golden calf was an Egyptian god, not one of the Israelites'. They had gotten accustomed to seeing animals worshipped where they lived. Are we, too, picking up the golden calves of our culture and putting them on our altars?

Jimmy Bakker recently confessed in his autobiography, *I Was Wrong*, that he had begun worshipping "the god of prosperity"—turning it into a golden calf. Many Christians worship "success in business," or "self-righteousness," far more than they worship the God Jesus knew and spoke of. The Pharisees' altars were so polluted with false gods that Jesus said their altars were really tombs full of old, filthy bones.

At a worship service in Philadelphia, the congregants together read aloud this prayer:

A Prayer for Coming Home

O True and Ever-Living God
I repent of all my false and empty gods
I look again into the closets of my life,
my mind, my heart
to see what rules me.
Whom do I serve?
What are the possessions,
the people, the opinions,
the events
that control my life?

O Welcoming One
I see you standing at the door
of my heart
waiting for me
You gaze at my strange gods
with an eye of compassion.
I am ashamed to invite you
into my cluttered house
yet my heart aches
to be at home with you.

My hand is reaching for the door
I hear myself saying, Come on in,
I have more room than I thought I had.
Come on in, and be the only God in my life.
May this moment of homecoming last forever.
— ANONYMOUS

Jesus kept his altar clean, worshipping not money or popularity or comfort or fame. Every day and every night he carefully swept it off, saying, "Dear God—I want only you." "Thou shalt have no other gods before me."—Deuteronomy 5:7

Jesus kept his altar clean.

Question

Draw a picture of an altar. Now sketch the answer to this question: What is on your altar?

Question

What do you have to do to keep your altar clean?

Question

What has to be taken off, and why?

Power Connection:

Dear Lord, my altar is so full right now I can hardly see Your face. If You came physically into my life, at the moment I'm not sure I could fit You into my calendar. Help me take whatever time or energy or space is needed to clean my altar today. Give me the grace and power to keep it clean, no matter how many truckloads of false gods and priorities back up daily to my door. Help me put all my activities in their proper place, keeping my altar clean for You.

Amen.

I, _____, keep my altar clean.

He Let Them Howl

A philosopher once said, "Do the thing and let them howl."

Jesus knew how unpopular some of his decisions were going to be with others, yet he let them howl. "Why do you concern yourselves with the approval that comes from man but do not worry about the approval that comes from God?" —John 5:44. Let them howl.

Judas cried, "Jesus, she's wasted her money." Pontius Pilate said, "You don't know how much power I have here." The Pharisees said, "You are from the devil himself." Peter said, "Don't go into Jerusalem!" In each of these circumstances, Jesus chose to let them howl. —John 12:5; John 19:16; Matthew 9:34; Matthew 16:23

"Let them howl" is a very challenging principle to follow, especially if the howling is from wolves circling your door or if, by reason of training or predisposition, you are conditioned to stop people from howling. Women have a particularly difficult time with this concept. We are socialized to stop the crying whenever it happens, and no matter where it comes from. (A nursing mother's breasts will lactate automatically when *any* baby cries—even if it's not her own.) No wonder it is difficult for women to let others howl. Yet there are times when we have to let howling continue so we can be about more important tasks—like sleep, for instance, or in the case of Joan of Arc, leading a nation to victory.

A friend of mine who was facing some challenging decisions in her company was worried about a particularly vocal group of critics. I asked her, "How will the critics react if you do what needs to be done?" "They will yell to the heavens," she solemnly assured me. "And what will their response be if you don't take the necessary action?" I asked. She thought a moment, and then answered, "They will yell anyway. In fact I'm beginning to think they just love the sound of their own howling." We both laughed in unison, "So, let them howl!"

Proverbs 18:2 states, "A rebel doesn't care about the facts. All he wants to do is yell."

When I was writing my first book a number of negative inner voices and fears began to surface. As I shared them with a counselor she began to smile. "Excellent, excellent," she murmured. "The more afraid you are, the better!" "Why?" I asked, almost angry at the casual way she was treating my night sweats. "Because, until the inner critics start to howl, you haven't hit the big leagues. Now we can be sure that you're on a larger playing field."

I recently learned that howler monkeys are the loudest animals in the jungle. They are not, however, the most powerful.

Jesus probably met with few complaints when he turned water into wine. He was, after all, just improving their drinking. But when he turned their system upside down, that's when they began to howl, because now he was affecting their *thinking.*

"Your approval or disapproval means nothing to me." —John 6:41

He let them howl.

Question

Who will howl if you do what you know needs to be done?

Question

When have you allowed others or your fears to howl in the past and been glad you did?

Question

What other famous leaders in history also "let them howl"?

Power Connection:

Dear Lord, help me not be influenced by the critical howls of others. Help me follow You step by step and trust that You and Your staff will keep the wolves away from Your currently fragile lamb. Help me realize that sometimes howling is part of the birthing process, but that joy and a new life will be the result.

Amen.

I, _____, let them howl.

He Went Looking for
What Was Lost

Jesus recited many parables about people searching for what was lost, like the widow who lost her penny under the floorboards and couldn't sleep until it was found, the shepherd who had ninety-nine sheep in the fold and went out in the rain to get the one that had wandered away, and the father waiting at the end of the road, scanning the horizon every day for the son who had been lost. All of these biblical illustrations point to the significance of the human search.

We must go looking for what is missing—we must go looking for what is lost. In Ezekiel 34, God makes very clear his desire to have shepherds who do their job and his anger at those who do not. "You haven't taken care of the weak nor bound up the broken bones nor gone looking for those who wandered away and are lost." —Ezekiel 34:4 (*The Living Bible*)

Instead, we are all too intent on "taking care of our-

selves, wearing the finest clothes, and eating the best meat."
God continues with a warning we all should heed. "I will hold
you responsible for what has happened to my flock." Ezekiel
34:10 (*The Living Bible*)

In Italy I was shocked to discover the scores of mangy
dogs that inhabit the ruins of Pompeii. At the entrance are
neatly lettered signs that read, "Do not touch the dogs." Before the forty-minute tour begins the guides are careful to instruct tourists not to touch the dogs. One look at the poor
animals and it is obvious why. They are covered with disease.
Yet they follow the tourists and lie down in the shadows of
the ancient temple. I was fascinated by the ruins, but haunted
by the dogs, wondering, *Why doesn't somebody take care of
them? They need medication and attention.* Evidently, there is
no humane society in Pompeii. There is no interest in looking for or caring for lost dogs.

In contrast, I must confess that I have walked through
the streets of New York (or Washington, D.C., or Philadelphia) and literally stepped over people sleeping in the door-
ways as I made my way to the shopping mall. I had not been
as haunted by them as I was by those uncared-for animals. I
learned on that same tour that foreigners perceive Americans
as being complacent about the homeless situation in our
country. One Australian told me he was shocked to find all
the homeless people in New York, wandering around un-
cared for. We have, unfortunately, grown accustomed to see-

ing homeless people in America. Too many of us have ceased looking for what has been lost.

At the State of the World Forum in San Francisco, I met a Catholic Buddhist monk from Cambodia. (As he explained it, there is no conflict in being a Catholic and a Buddhist, for "Catholicism is a religion, while Buddhism is a science.") As we were talking I asked him how he ended up in Cambodia. It seems that while he was walking to the immigration office in San Francisco he passed by the Cambodian refugee camp. A woman was wailing and hurling herself against the fence, so he went to see what the problem was. She held up a picture of a two-year-old child, and explained through her sobs that in the rush and crush of the crowd running for the boats she had been separated from her little girl. After a search through the camp she discovered that the child was not there, and she was beside herself, not knowing if she'd ever find her daughter. "What did you do?" I asked him. He said, "I promised that I would find her." "Did you?" I asked. "Yes," he replied. "Where?" I inquired. "In Cambodia." "How long did it take you to find her?" I continued. "Two years," he answered. "Two years!?" I exclaimed. "How did you locate her?" "I took the child's picture with me, and walked from village to village." "What about your other work?" I asked. "That *was* my work," he quietly replied. He then turned to introduce me to the friend sitting beside him, and that was the end of the conversation.

I wonder what kind of tasks we would have, if "searching for what was lost" were *our* only work. What would we be looking for?

Jesus said, "Father, these were your gifts to me. And I have not lost any of them." —John 17:12

Jesus went looking for what was lost.

Question

What has been lost in our country? In our culture?

Question

What has been lost in your life that you must now go searching for?

Question

What has God given or assigned to you that you have lost?

Question

When, and how, will your search begin?

Power Connection:

Dear Lord, You never lost me, even when I strayed into the briars and brambles. Give me the spirit of the good shepherd, who cannot sleep when even one lamb is missing. Help me understand what has been lost in our values, our culture, our churches, our synagogues, temples, and our country. Cause me to go diligently searching until that which is lost is found. In Your name I pray.

Amen.

I, _____, go looking for what is lost.

He Locked on to His Destiny

Anyone who has played computer games or watched movies that show pilots about to deploy missiles knows what it is to "lock on" to a target. The equipment and radar and homing devices have fixed their coordinates to keep the target in perfect range. At that point, all the pilot has to do is fire, because when the target has been "locked on to," the missile cannot miss.

Jesus used that same kind of focus to lock on to his destiny. He kept God's will and mission for his life always in view, and refused to let the pull and distractions and attractions of the world cause him to lose sight of his target. When he said, "It is finished," he was acknowledging that his destiny had been fulfilled. He had locked on to it, without wavering, and the mission was completed.

Many of us enjoyed the exploits of the young American

archer Justin Huish who won two Olympic gold medals in the sport. On one of the evening talk shows he performed a demonstration. His target had been set up through a garage and behind a flame and two waving balloons that seemed to block his view. The young man with the backward baseball cap and stylish sunglasses pulled his bow back as far as it would go, closed one eye, and then "locked on" to the target. He hit the bull's-eye. What he *hadn't* been focusing on was the garage, the flame, or the waving balloons. In his mind's eye there was nothing between him and that target. The destination was all he saw.

We would be more successful in achieving our life goals if we locked on to them with the young archer's concentration, and the precision of the military intelligence homing devices. Yet all too many of us would rather write reports on the size and length of the garage walls, the temperature of the flames, and the odds against hitting a target with obstructed vision.

To lock on to your destiny means you don't even see what's between you and it. Obstructions may be there, but they are not the object of your focus. You don't see *to* them, you see *through* them, when you are locked on.

Of course, in order to lock on to your destiny, you have to know or sense what it is. Jesus was certain about his; many of us are not so certain about ours. I addressed this subject at length in my book *The Path: Creating Your Mission Statement for Work and for Life*. The point of that book is that there is a divine destiny for us all—if we will be bold enough to believe it, and go searching for it.

More times than we realize God wants for us the very things that we deeply desire within our hearts, yet are too timid to claim. Our wavering hinders him from firing, if you will. We change our focus so often that there's no target even in sight, much less one that is clearly in view.

Jesus often asked people, "What do you want?" The ones who answered him got what they asked for. Jesus didn't feel it was his job to "guess" about people's desires.

When Jesus rebuked one of his best friends, Peter, for trying to keep him from going to Jerusalem, it was because he had already locked on to his destiny. Peter was trying to change the focus, yet Jesus guarded it adamantly. When his mother and family tried to urge him to come home again, he guarded his focus adamantly. When they questioned him as a twelve-year-old about why he had caused the family so much grief by staying behind and "getting lost" at the temple, he answered (in effect), "Don't be concerned about me, Mom and Dad. I'm locking on to my destiny."—Luke 2:42–49

Have you ever observed a cat leap from the floor to a ledge five feet above it? Its tail begins to twitch, it crouches down to gather its strength, and its eyes lock on to its destination—staring at the landing spot as if there were nowhere else for it to go. And then it leaps with such apparent ease that you forget the same feat would be impossible for a human being. Cats know something about focus that we have not yet learned. They know how to "lock on" to their destination with every fiber of their being.

"I know where I am going." —John 8:14

Jesus locked on to his destiny.

Question

Do you have your destiny in your sights?

Question

Is it locked in, or is it still fading in and out or bouncing around?

Question

What do you need to do to lock on to it?

Question

What is keeping you from locking on?

Power Connection:

Dear Lord, help me get my destiny clearly in focus. Help me set You and Your will in my sights, without wavering. Help me not to see the obstructions and distractions that surround my target, but keep my eyes always focused on it.

Amen.

I, _____, lock on to my destiny.

He Gave Them a Spirit of Redemption

To redeem means to save, to buy back, to recover. To redeem also means to "make good," as in "to redeem a coupon." We need a spirit of redemption, rather than a spirit of condemnation, to function in this world successfully. Having a spirit of redemption means that we can operate under the belief that we will receive what was promised, as well as have an assurance that even what we've lost by error can be "redeemed."

As victorious as King David was in his exploits, he did lose at least one battle. And he lost it not through being on the losing side, but by not being present at the battle at all. It seems that while he had been in one place fighting a skirmish, the enemy deployed part of its forces to go and capture the families and territory he had left undefended. When he returned home and discovered to his horror that he had been outsmarted, and worse, that his wife and children had been seized, he prayed that God would help him redeem the situation. "David engaged and fought them from dusk until the evening of the next day. David recovered everything the Amalekites had taken. Nothing was missing, young or old, boy or girl, plunder or anything else they had taken. David brought everything back." —1 Samuel 30:17–19 (*New International Version*). It is for this reason that he so often referred to God as his "redeemer." He was saying, "Even when I err, Lord, you can redeem the situation. In your compassion and wisdom and mercy, you can make this situation good again." David called God "My Rock and my Redeemer." — Psalm 19:14

One of my favorite examples of someone giving others a spirit of redemption concerns a priest named Father Arturo. One day he sent out an invitation to all the divorced people in his parish, announcing a special meeting on Thursday night. Many people came, curious about what this young priest had to say to them. He gathered them all in a room, asked them to be seated, and then knelt and began to wash their feet, asking forgiveness from them for the Church's hardness of heart.

What this young priest was doing was giving these people a spirit of redemption—telling them by this one act that they were redeemed through God's saving grace, and praying also that the Church would be redeemed from its judgemental, un-Christlike ways.

Elizabeth Anderson, director of the I Am Free Foundation, is working diligently to give a spirit of redemption to those in prison. She says that recent statistics show that by the year 1999, one in every ninety-nine citizens in the United States will have served time in prison. She therefore takes her work very seriously. She believes that the roots of crime are low self-esteem, and that prisoners must be shown new ways to heal and grow. Since only fifteen percent of the current prison population are hard-core professional criminals, she works to educate and inspire those other eighty-five percent so they can go on to lead productive lives. She is giving prisoners a spirit of redemption.*

The entire gospel, or "Good News" of Jesus is that we can be and have been redeemed. That each of our sad stories can have a happy ending, and that God's will for us involves an ultimate celebration, not on-going suffering and sorrow.

This theme permeates passages like Esther 9:22, which reads: "This was a time to remember when the Jews' sorrow was turned into joy, and their mourning into a day of celebration."

The prophet Isaiah came specifically to give people a spirit of redemption. Consider his poetic, prophetic words. The entire Chapter 35 of Isaiah is entitled "The Joy of the

---

*Contact I Am Free Foundation, 1750 Kalakaua Avenue, Suite 3535, Honolulu, HI 96826.

Redeemed." In Chapter 51:7–10 he writes, "How beautiful on the mountain are the feet of those who bring good news, who proclaim peace, who bring good tidings, who proclaim salvation, who say to Zion 'Your God reigns.'

"Listen! Your watchmen lift up their voices; together they shout for joy. When the Lord returns to Zion they will see it with their own eyes. Burst into songs of joy together, you ruins of Jerusalem, for the Lord has comforted his people, he has redeemed Jerusalem."—Isaiah 51:7

Surely few of us have had all the accumulated losses and woes of Job, yet "After Job had prayed for his friends, the Lord made him prosperous again and gave him twice as much as he had before. The Lord blessed the latter part of Job's life *more than the first.*"—Job 42:10–12 (*New International Version*)

Job, David, Isaiah, Jeremiah, confidently proclaimed throughout their lives "I know that my *Redeemer* lives."

Jesus gave us a spirit of redemption.

Question

What situation in your life right now needs to be redeemed?

Question

How would you function if you knew that the air you were surrounded by was infused by a spirit of redemption?

Question
How can you give others a spirit of redemption?

Power Connection:
Dear Lord, please help me remember Your spirit of redemption when I make a mistake or suffer a loss. Help me know that all form is temporary, and You are able through Your mercy and all knowingness to make even the most disastrous situation turn out to Your glory. Help me give others a spirit of redemption, too, that we all may grow in grace and gracefulness.

Amen.

I, _____, give a spirit of redemption.

He Leaned into the Kisses

Itook the nine-month-old child in my arms and said I'd gladly watch him as his mother ran an errand. The baby was quiet and seemed happy enough to gaze out on the other children playing all around. Enchanted by his long eyelashes, and drawn by the smell of his sweet baby's breath, I gently kissed the side of his head. He grew very still for a moment, and then leaned his head back toward my lips. I kissed him again. There was a momentary pause, as if he was soaking up the last kiss, and then he leaned again toward my kiss with great deliberation.

Having baby-sat other children whose reaction to affection was often a shy or petulant jerking away, I was delighted that this baby "leaned into the kisses." He was freely accepting tenderness when it was offered.

Jesus, too, leaned into the kisses. He was delighted to receive the embraces of children. He was deeply moved when

208

Mary anointed his feet. He did not push her away, saying as Judas did, "Oh, you shouldn't have done that. That oil could have been sold and the money given to the poor."—John 12:6. Jesus was signaling to us that even God is eager and hungry for affection freely given. He leaned into the kisses.

One of my poems reads, "Do you know what the cross says to me? That God would rather die than be without us." I am convinced that God wants our tenderness and our little love songs and our nicknames and our meaningless conversation. Can you imagine how you would respond to someone who only came to you asking for things . . . who only approached you with a solemn face, or a wailing sound, or a whining tone? Sure, you might fulfill their requests, but would you invite them to your parties?

That is why, I believe, Jesus leaned into the kisses. They felt so sweet and were so rare during the times when only fear or ambition dominated the thoughts of the people in the room. How nice it must have felt to him when somebody wanted just to give him kisses, asking nothing else in return.

A friend of mine says that God reveals his presence to her in many ways, and one of them is with white butterflies. Whenever a white butterfly appears she believes God is kissing her. She leans into the kisses. I found her example familiar because God speaks to me through ladybugs. I have found ladybugs on me or around me during some of the most trying, difficult times in my life—some even in winter. They have shown up in laundry rooms and on windshields, and one even landed on my nose as I was taking a nap. When I see a ladybug I lean into the kisses. I accept and believe that God is kissing me.

I've learned to accept compliments as evidences of God's kisses, as well as the many demonstrations of love and delight I am blessed to receive from others. Jesus said that we would receive power from on high, and I think the key word is "receive," which means to accept, to embrace, to lean into . . . the kisses.

I remember all too well times I did not lean into the kisses. My grandfather, a former State Hall of Fame basketball coach, had been reduced through age and illness to being homebound before he died. In order to keep busy he would shell pecans. When I would come to visit him he would offer me unlimited sacks of hand-shelled pecans. But I said, "No thanks, Grandpa. I don't like pecans." My thought was for him to save them for someone who would appreciate them, but in retrospect I realized the error of my ways. His pecans were his kisses, and I had pulled away, rather than receiving them.

Too many of us are so shortsighted and self-centered that we miss the kisses surrounding us. "This generation seeks a sign from God," Jesus sighed.—Mark 8:12. But we are missing all the kisses from the lilies in the fields, and especially from one another.

God is yearning to communicate with us in so many ways. Jesus received the children's hugs and flowers. "Oh yes, *let* the children come unto me," he said, kneeling down with open arms.—Matthew 19:14

He leaned into the kisses.

Question

How does God kiss you?

Question

How do you lean into the kisses?

Question

How, and when, do you turn away from "kisses"?

Power Connection:

Dear Lord, help me receive the affection You are eager to shower on me. Help me not keep score of what I want and need, but rather spontaneously lean into the kisses You offer in so many ways.

Amen.

I, _____, lean into the kisses.

Power

❧ ⚘

You will receive power from on high. —Luke 24:49

power: (pou'er) n., v., —n. 1. ability to do or act, capability of doing or accomplishing something 2. political or national strength 3. great or marked ability to do or act; strength, force 4. the possession of control or command over others, authority, ascendancy, influence

(Random House Webster's College Dictionary)

I experience power in its raw form when the airplane's engines begin their ultimate thrust and the wheels fold under its big silver belly and we are suddenly lifted into the air after speeding down a runway at hundreds of miles per hour. One second on the ground, the next in the sky—because of power. I also experience power when I am riding my quarterhorse stallion. We can be going along at a steady pace, him noticing everything with his eyes and ears, when suddenly a slight urging from my voice causes him to explode into a run that leaves both of us breathless, exalting. One minute walking on the ground, the next consuming it—because of power.

Jesus came to give us transformative power—to teach us how to experience it ourselves, and how to share it with others. "Why are you at the affect of this disease?" he questioned. "Take up your pallet and walk!" "Why do you remain chained to the past? Hear the new testament of my power!" "Never fear death again. You will live forever in my name!" Jesus told his bewildered disciples to wait and pray together until power came—until they could see and feel the tongues of flame God's Holy Spirit would bring them.

Power. We all seek it. Jesus came to show us where, and how, it truly can be found.

He Said,
"Take It Out of This"

Several of my closest friends and I had a retreat we often went to outside Yuma, Arizona, called Gold Rock Ranch. Each of us was a highly involved business professional who felt the stresses of constantly having to perform and "look good," so the rules out at Gold Rock Ranch were that you couldn't wear anything that matched, no phones were allowed, and the main basis of exchange among us was rocks that we found on our hikes through the desert. As we were sitting by the fire one night, we started talking about how we loved the scenes in the Western movies where a cowboy would saunter up to the bar, order a whiskey, and then toss a leather pouch full of gold nuggets down and say with a steely glare, "Here—take it out of this." We got such a kick out of that image that Willy made each of us leather pouches that we filled with "gold nuggets" (our small but highly prized rocks). We'd walk over to one another, ask for a drink, throw the pouch down, and then say with the requisite glare, "Here—take it out of this."

All of us ultimately have to be able to say, "Here—take it out of this." Because we are constantly being challenged about the depth and breadth of our resources, we have to know exactly how many gold nuggets are in our pouch and what they weigh. We have to know what is ours.

When questioned about how he was going to pay Caesar's tax, Jesus told one of his disciples to go find a fish. Sure enough, a fish was caught with a coin in his mouth. Jesus might have told Andrew to deliver the tax and say, "Here, Caesar. Take it out of this!" —Matthew 17:27. Likewise, when asked how he was going to feed a crowd of 5,000 people, Jesus looked at the five loaves and two fish and said gleefully, "Here—take it out of this!" —Matthew 14:17

When David went to meet Goliath he used the gold nuggets of his previously successful experiences to know that he could bring down a lion or a giant. When he ran toward Goliath declaring his faith he was saying (in effect), "Here, Goliath, take it out of *this!*" —1 Samuel 17:44–48

When Moses went to meet Pharaoh he asked God, "Who shall I say is sending me?" And God said, "Tell them I Am is sending you." —Exodus 3:14. So Moses put that nugget of authority in his pouch and marched up to Pharaoh and said, "Let my people go." When Pharaoh laughed at him, Moses raised his miracle producing staff and said (in effect), "Here— Pharaoh. Take it out of this." —Exodus 7:10

"All that the Father has is mine." —John 16:15
Jesus said, "Take it out of this."

Question
What are the gold nuggets or resources in your pouch?

Question
What would you like to order with confidence?

Question
From what or whom do you get your authority?

Power Connection:
Dear Lord, You have given me Your name and authority to use with confidence and for good. Help me claim my rightful standing in You. Help me remember that all You have is mine, and I am Yours. Help me pray with confidence, lead with confidence, and direct others with confidence, knowing Your love and Your calling are the only authority I need.
Amen.

I, _____, say, "Take it out of this."

He Created Openings

Anyone who has experience in sales and marketing knows this feeling: You're in a dark place. You're tied up in knots. You've got to break through with a sale, an idea, an exciting concept, or you will be fired, killed, destroyed, or even worse—*humiliated*. Yet somehow, you create an opening. The phone call gets through. The meeting takes place. The contract gets signed. The sale gets made, and you are singing the *Hallelujah Chorus* rather than a funeral dirge. You created an opening.

Jesus created openings—most memorably when he escaped the sealed tomb. The entire gospel is about the miraculous power we have been given to look at places that seem sealed shut and create openings. Paul and Timothy were in prison until the angels came to help them create an opening. The Israelites were at a stunned standstill, facing a raging sea, until God through Moses created an opening.

Sally went to Atlanta without a job, confident that she would find something in the city she had longed to live in. She took a job with a temporary agency, wanting to create income immediately and also to get to know the town. On her second assignment the supervisor was so impressed with her work that she asked her to stay on. Sally asked, "As what?" And the supervisor replied, "I don't know. We'll create an opening." Sally had such an infectious enthusiasm and such a professional approach to the problems at hand that the supervisor made an opening for her when there was no opening. Sally literally just had to show up, and a job was invented for her. Her faith created the opening.

World-famous movie director and producer Steven Spielberg launched his career by showing up on the movie studio lot—being so eager to be a part of that world that he would just hang out there every day. Eventually, someone gave him a job, and the rest is Academy Award–winning history. Steven Spielberg created an opening for himself by his presence and his passion.

When I began expanding my advertising agency, I hired two salespeople. One sat at his desk and began methodically contemplating how to write a plan to begin to do "cold calling." The other got out the phone book and started chuckling triumphantly in her office. When I asked her what she was so happy about, she held up the Yellow Pages and said, "Look at this. Every one of the people in here needs our services. I just have to go out and tell them about us!" Guess which salesperson had the outstanding sales? Frenchie's faith created openings everywhere. During her first week she brought in three substantial accounts.

Powerful people are not paid to waltz through existing openings. Our job is to create new ones. Don't look at a situation and say it cannot be penetrated. *Create* an opening. The only two tribes that made it into the Promised Land were those of Joshua and Caleb. They were the ones who saw past the giants into the grapevines and fig trees. They declared boldly, "It is a very good land, full of promise. With God's help, we will create the openings!"—Numbers 13:30. Sure enough, they were the ones who went in.

"The angel said to the woman, "Do not be afraid, for I know you are looking for Jesus, who was crucified. He is not here; he has risen, just as he said. Come and see the place in the tomb where he lay."—Matthew 28:5

Jesus created openings.

Question
What situation looks impenetrable right now?

Question
Who might help you create an opening?

Question
What are other situations in scripture where God created openings?

Dear Lord, the situation before me right now looks like a solid rock of resistance. Help me create an opening. Help me not view the situation as anything other than an opportunity for another victory in You. Help me, like You, escape this seemingly sealed up tomb, and go on to have a picnic with the ones I love.

Amen.

I, _____, create openings.

He Connected the Dots

The solving of puzzles or problems is often a matter of connecting the dots. Many times all the clues are there for us, but we have not made the necessary connections. We must learn to look for the larger picture, and then see patterns emerge from there. Sometimes we have to go beyond the dots in order to connect them, as the infamous exercise of "connect these dots without lifting your pen" teaches us. (In this exercise, one has to go outside the dots and come in from a steep angle high above them in order to connect them all with one stroke.)

In a recent study on problem solving, experts analyzed twenty of the world's most recent and innovative creations, ranging from Liquid Paper to the Sony Walkman. They studied the people involved to see if there was a pattern that could be duplicated. The only two characteristics they found in common among these creative people were these: All had a terrific sense of humor, and all had a high tolerance for clutter. The high tolerance for clutter means that creators are able to mentally filter the core ideas or values, and are able to connect the dots that are seemingly scattered around the room.

Humor has been called the ultimate form of bi-sociative thinking, because with humor one has to look at a situation in two ways—seeing the facts as they are, *and* finding the humor in them. I will always be grateful for the games my parents taught us to play around the dinner table. One on-going game we played was "What was the funniest thing that happened to you today?" Each of us got to share some event, and it quickly taught us to look for the humor in things so we'd have something funny to say at the dinner table. I can remember laughing so hard at one of my sister's stories that I actually snorted a pea up my nostril. Then that became the funny story and you see how it goes. My parents were teaching us to connect each day's dots to our funny bone.

Another "connect the dot" game I was grateful for growing up was one my grandfather taught me. He would take me on walks and pick up a rock and say, "What do you see in this?" I would say, "A rock, Granpa," and he would say "Look again." I was amazed at how he could see a cowboy hat, a spoon, or, if you turned the rock this way, a puppy dog. It taught me, though, to look for larger patterns—to try to see how certain lines or dots connected with other ones in interesting ways. (The paneling in my mother's guest room keeps me up at night, because I see elephants and horses and monkeys and ballerinas all dancing in the swirls of wood. I can't help but connect the dots.)

Consultants are really highly paid experts who specialize in dot connecting. People hire them to see the patterns that they themselves may be too close to to see. Diagnosticians connect the dots between different tests and medical data. The act of neurons leaping from one synapse to another constitutes the act of thought itself. If the dots are not connected, a thought does not occur.

When Jesus took all the laws and the prophecies and explained them in simple stories, he was connecting the dots for us. As he spoke, we began to see the pattern emerging of God's love.

"Seek *first* the kingdom of heaven, and all else will be added unto you."—Matthew 6:33

Jesus connected the dots.

Question

Think for a moment about a problem that is concerning you. What dots could you look beyond that might show you the pattern of the bigger picture?

Question

How often do you connect the dots of life to your funny bone?

Power Connection:

Dear Lord, with each puzzling situation before me, help me connect the dots. Give me Your wisdom to see the relationships between various pieces of information, and make intuitive leaps that lead me to truth and wisdom.

Amen.

I, _____, connect the dots.

Amen

He Did a Pattern Interrupt

One therapeutic technique that has proven to be effective in certain situations is called a "pattern interrupt." This method is based on the theory that the mind seems to lay down physical grooves of memories, with one memory triggering another until soon, just one thought can trigger an entire chain. (In this regard, the mind is like the piano player who says, "Hum a few bars and I'll play the whole tune.") In its negative aspect, if you allow the memory-sequence chain to just keep playing, you can end up with a diatribe of negative or painful recollections that then becomes a monologue of grief, depression, or self-pity. If that occurs frequently, it may be time for "a pattern interrupt."

A pattern interrupt is any unanticipated action or behavior that is seemingly unrelated to the activity that was previously taking place. Being under pressure at work and suddenly throwing a party, for example, would be a pattern interrupt. Interrupting a boring conversation by knocking over a glass of water and suddenly breaking out singing your high school anthem would be a pattern interrupt. Walking up and hugging your enemy would be a pattern interrupt. Dropping your voice to a whisper while everyone else is shouting would be a pattern interrupt. Children are marvelous at doing pattern interrupts, especially if they see a parent advancing with a scowl and decide to change the subject, or to tell Mommy how pretty she is today.

Jesus did a major "pattern interrupt." He stopped all the sad songs of gloom and doom and said, "Enough! The Messiah has come. *Now* what are you going to complain about?"

Dr. Seuss tells a story about a character that gets into THE WAITING ZONE and cannot find a way out. It just keeps waiting and waiting. It hangs around people who are waiting. Like the characters in the play *Waiting for Godot*, these people are waiting for someone who never comes. People who like to wait need a pattern interrupt. He interrupted their patterns of procrastination.

In studying the lives of some of my favorite creative geniuses, I found that often when they got into a slump they would take a trip. Walt Disney found much of his inspiration from trips abroad. "It's a small world after all." Georgia O'Keeffe was painting dark cityscapes until someone suggested she visit the Southwest. The pastel desert scenery was a sharp pattern interrupt to her gray, severe city scenes, and she achieved greatness sharing her newly discovered beauty with us. When Saul was on the road to Damascus, intent on destroying as many Christians as he could find, he got knocked off his ass (literally) and was blinded for three days. It was a direct result of this major "pattern interrupt" that the world's most famous evangelist—Paul—found his calling.—Acts 9:1–30

We are such creatures of habit that it is easy to become enslaved to old ways of thinking. Sometimes disease can be a pattern interrupt—reminding us that our time on earth is limited. People who have to engage in a lot of mental activity often find that "mindless" work like gardening can rejuvenate their whole beings. Workaholics who are in an obsessive-compulsive pattern may need a pattern interrupt if they are to gain balance. When family and friends do an intervention on someone they are doing a pattern interrupt—saying, in effect, "Your excesses are hurting us, and we aren't going to take it anymore."

Self-esteem counselor Diane Loomans recommends that one effective way to stop an argument is to put on a funny nose and mustache. She keeps two pairs handy, so that when one of the clients is out of control with anger, she can pop on her funny nose and give one to the client as well. Another technique she uses is to have both parties suddenly take each other's role. One person yells, "Switch," and then people are suddenly forced to see things from the other party's perspective. Both of these methods are interrupting a pattern.

Powerful people must have the "pattern interrupt" tool

in their repertoire. It can certainly redirect lives (as well as put an end to long and boring conversations).

One definition of insanity is to expect to get different results by doing the same old things.

"The day of salvation is *now*.—Luke 19:9

Jesus did a "pattern interrupt."

Question

What negative pattern currently has you in its grip?

Question

How can you do a pattern interrupt?

Question

When have you had a memorable "pattern interrupt" in your life?

Power Connection:

Dear Lord, You are a master at interrupting people's negative patterns. Help me recognize when I or others are in a downward spiral, so I, too, can initiate a valuable "pattern interrupt."

Amen.

I, _____, do a pattern interrupt.

He Had Saturation
Knowledge

Recently I saw a *National Geographic* special about a
writer/photographer who was assigned to do a story about
alligators in the Everglades. The reporter explained, "Rather
than write *about* alligators, I decided to try to become one."
After months of preparation this man went into the Everglades with his camera and *very carefully* walked into an area
of swamp that was heavily populated with alligators. The
only weapon he took with him was a two-foot-long stick. His
movements were slow and deliberate, and eventually he sank
down to eye level with the reptiles. He proceeded to stand
there patiently and observe them for hours, moving slowly
when they moved, going underwater when they went underwater, pushing them gently away with his stick when their
curiosity about him brought them within biting range. The
photographs he took of them from this perspective had never

been done before, and the insight he gained about their world made his writing a revelation rather than a mere report.

Jesus became one of us so that he could speak *to* us, not *at* us—with us, not beyond us. His becoming human indicates the highest level of interest possible—a study based not on ancient texts or the reconstruction of pottery fragments, but on drinking and partying and crying and sleeping and playing with us—on eating our bread and laughing at our jokes and wiping away our tears. This is how Jesus came to be with us. His knowledge of the human heart and condition was based on saturation knowledge. He knew us intimately, and thus he could speak with authority about our situations.

In the book *Intuition and Work*, John Renesch recounts how a consultant used saturation knowledge to help solve an engineering problem. It seems that live salmon were being injured in certain shipping processes. A thorough check of all the systems, however, showed nothing wrong. The engineers finally decided to "become the salmon" mentally, visualizing in detail and describing in writing what the process was like from a fish-eye point of view. After this exercise in saturated thinking, the problems were solved. Saturation thinking led to the realization that the fish were being traumatized by the handling *process*, even though the system's *design* looked flawless.

Too often leaders or managers who are brought in apply pet theories or formulas—and yet have never had any practical, real-world experience. One CEO I know, Ken, met with a manager who presented a beautifully packaged and prepared report on what he thought the rural market needed. Ken looked at him and said, "I'm not even going to read this until I see the mud." "What mud?" the young man replied. "The mud on your boots from walking those fields," Ken replied. "I don't want to hear from you about rural markets until you can tell me which brand of beer they drink and what their kids do after school and what the neighbors talk about after church and the colors of the high school football team." "But, Ken," the man protested, "these formulas are based on sound research." "Mud!" Ken bellowed. "I want to see *their* mud on *your* boots!" Then he paused and asked, "John, do you even own a pair of boots?" "No," John murmured bashfully. "I didn't think so," said Ken. "Get out of my office and come back when you do." Ken then turned to me and exclaimed in amazement, "And he wants to tell us about rural markets?"

Some cities require the municipal engineers to try to navigate downtown areas in wheelchairs. Some nursing homes require their aides to smear Vaseline on their glasses and stuff cotton in their ears so they will know what it is like to try to see and hear clearly through the effects of aging. My friend Deb shared with me her surprise when they got the photos developed that her three-year-old daughter had taken with the camera they gave her. "Laurie, all she had was photographs of kneecaps!" Deb laughed. We cannot see the world through a child's eyes without getting on our knees and looking at things the way they do. We, too, must get saturation knowledge.

Getting saturation knowledge means soaking yourself, surrounding yourself, diving into and swimming around in the atmosphere, feelings, currents, and trends as well as just the facts. Saturation knowledge means *heart* knowledge about a situation. Too many of us just seek the bare facts and think we have all the information we need.

If you're having problems with your teenager, "become" your teenager for a few days. Try as much as possible to listen to his music, or watch her videos, or do her homework. Write down the input they are receiving at every level, and try to process it yourself. Become your own customer for a day, receiving the same kind of treatment, service, credit, and shipping arrangements.

In other words, don't look "at" your problem, *look out at the world from inside it.* This is the perspective you'll get from obtaining saturation knowledge.

"When Jesus had finished teaching, the crowds were amazed, for he spoke as one who had authority, and not as the scribes."—Matthew 7:28–29

Jesus had saturation knowledge.

Question
    In what areas do you have saturation (heart as well as head) knowledge?

He Had Saturation Knowledge   233

Question

Based on your mission, in which areas should you get saturation knowledge?

Question

Are you willing to put in the time it takes to saturate yourself in your desired area of interest? If so, what could be the rewards—for you and for the people you would be serving?

Power Connection:

Dear Lord, help me get saturation knowledge in the areas of my mission. Let me soak up Your wisdom through my pores. Let me murmur Your thoughts day and night. Let me know Your mind, God, and Your heart. Saturate me with Your courage, Your power, and Your love.

Amen.

I, _____, get saturation knowledge.

He Opened the Gate

When I was a little girl, one of my favorite things to do was help my father with irrigation. Living in the valley, we had land that depended on water that would come down the canal at prescheduled times—sometimes as late as midnight. I would wait up with my dad, hoping that he might let me be the one to lift up the gate. I loved watching the sudden rush of water flow into the field. It once occurred to me that if the gate wasn't opened, the water would continue flowing by, unaccessed, although it was only a foot away from the thirsty land.

Jesus opened the gate. He, too, wanted to see the water rush into the fields. He literally *became* the gate so that God's love and blessings could flow into areas that had been lacking moisture for years.

A powerful person's job is to open the gate—to make new resources available to others—to bring an onrush of life-giving support to thoughts and ideas that others may have been thirsting for. We must know where vital resources are and where they will come from in the future, so as to make sure they are dispersed to all the right places. Powerful people's jobs are to open the gate to new possibilities.

Teachers can open the gate to knowledge. Preachers can open the gate to wisdom. Parents can open the gate to unlimited potential. Friends can open the gate to increased confidence and faith. We must begin to see ourselves as being gates for others. Imagine the person standing before you has no other access to God's love and blessing but you. Are you willing to open the gate?

Jesus was aware of all the resources in heaven. He knew that blessings were literally flowing by, unclaimed . . . unaccessed. He planted his feet firmly on the ground and became the gate, so that *all* the blessings from heaven could pour into the thirsty souls on earth.

He came to Nazareth, where he had been brought up, and went into the synagogue on the Sabbath as he usually did. He stood up to read, and they handed him the scroll of the prophet Isaiah. Unrolling the scroll he found the place where it is written:

The spirit of the Lord has been given to me
for he has anointed me,
He has sent me to bring the good news to the poor,

to proclaim liberty to captives,
and to the blind new sight,
to set the downtrodden free,
to proclaim the year of the Lord's favor."
—ISAIAH 61:1–2

He then rolled up the scroll, gave it back to the assistant, and sat down. All eyes in the synagogue were fixed on him. Then he began to speak to them, "This text is being fulfilled today even as you listen." —Luke 4:16–22

He opened the gate.

Question

What resources are flowing by you, unclaimed or unaccessed?

Question

How can you powerfully open the gate for others?

Question

Specifically, which gates will you open and how?

Power Connection:

Dear Lord, help me recognize all the blessings and knowledge and power that are flowing by the people, unaccessed because no one has opened the gate for them. Help me be a means of distributing Your resources to all who hunger and thirst for Your love.

Amen.

I, _____, open the gate.

He Stepped into the Water

Iloved going to the neighborhood pool the first day it opened every summer. I remember standing on the edge of the really, *really* tall diving board and wondering just how cold the water below would be. Those few "prejump" seconds seemed like an eternity. My friends behind me would begin banging on the board, shouting, "If you're not going to jump, get out of the way so we can!" Finally I would slowly step off the board, and summer would officially begin.

Jesus also stepped into the water. When he left Heaven to grow in the waters of his mother's womb, he stepped from being God to being also human, from a state of knowing to one of surrender. When he emerged from the womb and inhaled his first breath of earthly air, he once again changed atmospheres. He didn't cling to one environment, believing only there could he thrive.

In baseball we know that you can't run to home while your foot is still stuck on third base. Yet so many of us lose opportunities because we want to stay in "safe" territory. We want familiarity to ease the way, unrolling like a red carpet in front of us. Yet when God said, "Now," Jesus stepped into the waters and trusted.

Not long ago I was involved in presenting an opportunity to a group of physicians. Excited by the proposal, yet anxious about how it would turn out, they decided to "run it past the attorney." This, of course, created a six-month delay while the attorney changed two-syllable words into six-syllable "lawyerese." He urged in his final memorandum to the group to wait another year "to see which way the market went." After hearing both sides of the argument, one of the board members commented, "We know what this will cost us to do. My question is, 'What will it cost us *not* to act on this?' How can we ever measure the cost of a lost opportunity?" His passionate plea won the day, and the group engaged in launching what became a trend-setting campaign.

The group stepped into the water—going from a point of uncertainty to a point of willingness and surrender. They changed atmospheres.

When the Israelites were fleeing Egypt, they were brought up short by the Red Sea. God issued instructions to Moses, and when he led them into the water, land appeared.

Moses did not part the Red Sea by studying it from a distance. He had to be willing to get his feet wet before the *dry* land appeared.—Exodus 14:1–21

When Joshua was leading the Israelites into Canaan, God gave him very specific instructions. "When you have reached the brink of the waters of the Jordan, you are to stand still *in the Jordan itself.*" Then Joshua said, "As soon as the priests with the ark of the Lord have set their feet *in the waters of the Jordan*, the waters will be stopped in their course and stand still in one mass." —Joshua 3:7–13

Thousands of years later, Jesus, too, was instructed to step into the river Jordan's swirling waters, and when he emerged, he knew his life would never be the same.

"And straightway coming up out of the water, he saw the heavens opened, and the spirit like a dove descending on him."—Mark 1:10

Jesus stepped into the water.

Question
    What water is swirling before you, waiting for your first step?

Question
    If you have not already stepped into it, how long do you plan to just stand on the diving board?

Question

Do you think you can only thrive in a certain kind of atmosphere?

Power Connection:

Dear Lord, give me the courage to step into the rivers of change, because change means new opportunities and new openings for growth. Help me not linger forever on the diving board, or on the banks of the river, when Your voice is telling me to step into the water boldly.

Amen.

I, _____, step into the water.

He Gave Them a Clean Plate

In this country, it is not only improper—it is technically illegal to be served with a dirty plate. Salad bars post signs indicating that the Health Department *requires* that each time you step up to the buffet, you must do so with a clean plate. Besides, nobody in his right mind would eat on plates that have baked-on grunge. Yet every day many of us step up to God's banquet with a dirty plate, and then wonder why we aren't being served. Jesus, too, insists on a clean plate for everyone.

He was emphatic about the necessary cleansing power of forgiveness. He said, "Before you go to the altar, go and make peace with your brother." —Matthew 9:13. Do not come into my house with a dirty plate.

Jesus' power to wash others left no lingering germs or stains. Even Peter, three times a coward, got to move forward with new boldness and courage after Jesus absolved him. Peter got a clean plate.

In order to experience God's power fully, it is imperative that we let our family, friends, and coworkers start with a clean plate each day. Do we hold grudges, harbor resentments, carry over some *dis-ease* we had with them yesterday or last year? We are admonished not to let the sun set on our anger. In other words, wash the dishes before we go to bed.

We must start each day with a clean plate. Our plate is our conscience. Is it clean? Are there some unwashed portions—even on the underside? Our plate is our heart. Are we harboring grunge-filled resentments or clumps of baked-on anger as we continually ask for second helpings? Have we forgiven ourselves?

Jesus could not have motivated his team if he had not given each of them a clean plate. Former prostitute? No problem! You will become my example of precious, holy love. Former coward? No problem! You will become a legendary leader. Former skeptic? No problem! You, Paul, will go on to declare the Gospel in new and exciting ways. Clean plate. Clean plate. Clean plate.

The danger in having the grunge of resentment on your plate is the *poison* that can come from it. It has finally occurred to me that the only one hurt by my anger will be me. If I hold on to it, thinking the other person is being punished, I am wrong. Resentment is full of disease-causing germs.

That's why Jesus said we had to get rid of it—not only so the object of our anger could be set free, but more important, so we can.

Every one of the people Jesus worked with—those who walked forward—was given a new, bright robe of righteousness to wear and very clean feet. No leftover sins, unwashed resentment, half-baked disappointments, lingered on the plates he handed out, either.

"If I do not wash you, you have no part in me."—John 13:8

He gave everyone a clean plate.

Question
> Is your plate clean?

Question
> How- -and how often—do you wash it?

Question
> Have you given others a clean plate? If not, who, and why not?

Question
> When have others given you a clean plate?

Power Connection:

Dear Lord, help me wash everyone's plate clean. Help me recognize Your power to transform, save, redeem, and change even those who have hurt me the most. Let me not be a carrier of germs, a bearer of bad will, but let me give others good news of Your everlasting love and cleaner-than-clean forgiveness.

Amen.

I, _____, give them a clean plate.

He Was Authentic

An Old Testament prophet wrote, "The honest man gives his own conduct careful thought. He does not act a part in public."—Ecclesiasticus 1:29 (*New Jerusalem Bible*)

Jesus was the same person whether he was at a party or a political function. He was authentic, real. He was himself no matter who he was with or where he was. The authenticity of his personality was as attractive to people as the miracles he performed.

What was it that made him stand out in a crowd? He was probably of average height and build, and as the Scripture says, "There was nothing beautiful that we should desire him." —Isaiah 53:2. The thing that distinguished him was his authenticity. "If you have seen me," he said, "you have seen the Father." —John 14:9. In other words, "I am the real thing."

Although I enjoy dressing up in business suits and looking the part of the business executive, I feel most at home in my "cowboy getup," as my grandmother used to call it. (She loved to tell the tale about Mom's buying me a brand-new pair of jeans, and then my coming over with an old rope tied around the leg. I was five years old. "Why is that old rope tied around your leg, Laurie Beth?" asked my grandfather, amused. I said simply, "My pants are too new." After I grew up and moved back to the Southwest, I was walking through an old flea market–type store in New Mexico. I had just been working with the horses, and so I had on my old hat, blue jeans, and muddy boots. As I was wandering through the aisle I heard a voice call out, "Hey—are you for real?" I turned and in the dim light tried to make out the source of the voice. "Excuse me?" I asked. "I said, are you really like how you're dressed, or is that just for show?" "Oh, this is me, all right," I laughed, turning toward the back of the room. Out walked this old, old lady, holding up an incredible antique Mexican bridle. "I've been saving this for someone who could appreciate it," she said, carefully handing me her treasure. "I figured you might be for real."

"Hey, are you for real?" God calls out, sometimes from the darkness. "Are you really like you're dressed, or is that outfit just for show? Because if you're for real," he says, "I will bring out my treasures to share with you."

Authentic. Made by hand. Certified by the Creator. One of a kind. Antique glass has little waves in it, perceptible only when you stand and look at it a certain way. Real crystal pings when you tap it. Genuine pearls don't chip when they're bitten. Diamonds cut glass and not vice versa.

A friend of mine named Betty Ann is a delight to all who know her. A human dynamo of energy and brilliance, she is using her gifts to help make needed changes in the health care industry. She meets regularly with CEOs, accountants, and physicians who, by virtue of the turbulence in the industry, are not known for their sense of humor in business meetings. One day she was explaining to a gloomily silent group of executives why they needed to increase their nursing levels and consolidate their pharmacy departments in order to maximize efficiency and increase quality of care. One of them suddenly called out "You must be from Texas, Betty Ann." "Why," she asked, suddenly sniffing her armpits—"is it that obvious?" The group dissolved into laughter and the needed changes were discussed in a far less tense atmosphere. Everyone who knows Betty Ann verifies that she is one authentic human being.

In Isaiah 43:4 God speaks and says, "You are precious and honored in my sight, and I love you!" God created our authenticity. Why do we then struggle so much to be like others? "My inmost self rejoices when from your lips come honest words."—Proverbs 23:16

One of the ten commandments has to do with bearing false witness—or swearing to something that is false. I think it also applies to how we portray ourselves as well. God detests it when we swear to something that is false. "I hate, I detest delusion." —Psalm 119:163.

I wonder how many nervous breakdowns and failed marriages are caused because people hide or sacrifice their authenticity. Ralph Waldo Emerson warned that we should beware of any enterprise that requires us to buy new clothes. In a beautiful passage called "The Arrival," from the Egyptian Book of the Dead, the author speaks to the delight of the authenticity of the soul. He says, "Like a rabbit from the depth of its hutch, blinking at light, I have come. In my heart a lyre is humming. Its strings ring true. My body is rolled papyrus tied with red strings that hold no pretense. I spread the length of myself before friends and the gods and let them study me."*

"This is my Beloved Son, in whom I am well pleased."—Luke 3:22

Jesus was authentic.

Question

Where in your life are you being a phony? Why?

Question

Do you dress and act like who you want to be? Why or why not?

*Source: Timothy Freke, *Heaven* (Berkeley: Conari Press.)

Question

Describe a recent experience that brought out your authentic self.

Question

What is the value of seeking authenticity
- in yourself?
- in others?

Power Connection:

Dear Lord, help me love and cherish my authentic self. Help me to quit trying to squeeze into molds that do not suit me. May I never again allow myself to wear a pair of shoes that don't fit.

Amen

I, _____, am authentic.

He Had No Sense of Entitlement

Jesus easily and rightfully could have allowed himself to be waited on hand and foot from the day of his birth. By virtue of his birthright, he was entitled to the finest of everything. Yet rather than straightening and polishing his crown, he took it off. Instead he picked up the fisherman's net, the servant's washcloth, and the empty bucket at the well. He did not expect others to do for him what he was not willing to do for himself. He had no sense of entitlement. "Who, being in the form of God, did not count equality with God as something owed him, but instead he emptied himself, taking on the form of a servant." —Philippians 2:6–8

This notion of being "owed" something is the exact opposite of what Christ came to teach us.

It is not surprising that the portion of the federal budget that is threatening to bankrupt our country is called "entitlements". Sometime after World War II we, as a society, got the idea that the government was supposed to take care of us from the cradle to the grave, and we all have been paying for that notion ever since. We also are often called "ugly Americans" overseas because of an attitude that, because we are Americans, things should be done for us in a certain way, in a certain manner, and darn quickly, thank you.

Catherine has a friend who spends a great deal of time working with prisoners. She asked if I knew what one thing nearly all prisoners have in common. "What?" I asked. "The one thing all prisoners seem to have in common is an attitude that somebody *owes them*," she said.

Jesus knew that his inheritance in heaven was guaranteed, but he worked very hard to apprehend it and secure it here on earth. In the outstanding movie *Dead Man Walking*, the father of a murdered daughter tells Sister Helen Prejean that he wishes he had the faith she has. She looks at him and says softly, "Oh, it isn't faith. It's *work*."

The Christian mystery involves knowing that we are saved by grace and yet living as if our entry to heaven depended on our service to others. As a born-again believer for more than thirty years, I have long believed my place "in heaven" is secure. I was warned *against* resting on that crown, however, when a good friend wrote me and said, "Laurie, if I die first I'm going to be waiting for you in heaven. And *you'd better get there*," she underlined. I laughed, and then realized the seriousness of her message. None of us should have a sense of entitlement about heaven. Not when the needs on earth are so great.

We must be about the *work* of faith. We must take up the fishermen's nets and the empty buckets and the servants' washcloth. We would do far more for the world if we spent less time straightening our crowns and more time washing others' feet, just as Jesus did.

He had no sense of entitlement.

Question

Where do you display a sense of entitlement? Be honest.

Question

When and how have you taken off your crown and taken up the empty bucket?

Question

What do you feel each person is entitled to? What must we work for?

Power Connection:

Dear Lord, I know that You have given me all things— most important is Your love. Help me remember to follow the example of Jesus and be a *servant*, as well as your royal child.

Amen.

I, _____, have no sense of entitlement.

He Led Them with Cords of Kindness

I led them with cords of human kindness, with leading ties of love."—Hosea 11:4. I find it interesting that the word *cord* is used in this verse, because it implies something that is braided or woven. Deeds interwoven with attitudes of forgiveness, compassion, and gentleness are the threads that go into a "cord of kindness." Kindness doesn't sound like a very powerful word, does it? It doesn't seems to be in the same league with words such as *forcefulness*, *power*, or *authority*. Yet kindness is the way that Jesus chose to lead.

Scripture is filled with references to God's nature being a kind or merciful one. "What I desire is mercy, not sacrifice." —Matthew 9:13. "I will pour out a spirit of kindness and prayer." —Zechariah 12:10. "The cherubim faced each other, with outstretched wings that overshadowed the place of mercy, and looked down upon it." —Exodus 37:9. Your own soul is nourished when you are kind.—Proverbs 11:17

Jesus led his sheep with cords of kindness, yet many fear-based religions infer that God leads his flock with whips and chains. This is simply not true. Humans respond creatively more to kindness than intimidation.

Piero Soderini, a wise leader of the city of Florence, wrote the following letter of introduction to the Cardinal of Volterra, regarding a young artist named Michelangelo. "His manner is such that, if appropriately treated and addressed, he will do the impossible. Be generous towards him with kindness and affection, and he will accomplish things that will astonish the world."* It was in Florence that Michelangelo created David, and a number of other masterpieces.

When the phone would ring at night, yet was obviously someone calling the wrong number, my mother would say, "I'm sorry. You've misdialed. Who were you looking for?" And then she'd listen and say, "Well, have you tried finding them in the Yellow Pages? Or perhaps you might try Information." I said to her one evening, "Mom, why don't you just hang up?" And she said, "Well, honey, they were intent on finding someone they obviously needed to talk to. I thought maybe I could help." Such a fine thread of kindness was one of many she would weave each day.

One of my fondest memories is sitting in a field of wild-flowers high atop the Swiss Alps. It was a summer's day, and in the distance you could see the snowcapped peaks piercing

*Marie-Ange Guillame, *Tuscany* (New York, London, Paris: Abbeville.)

the clouds. Down below lay beautiful Lake Lucerne. As I lay there relaxing, the slightest tinkling of cowbells floated up the valley. The more I tuned into it the more I began to hear this subtle symphony echoing throughout the hills. I learned later that each local farmer puts bells on the cows so he can always know where they are, even when he can't see them. And at evening, when it's time to lead them home, he takes a wreath of flowers and puts it across the shoulders of the cow that has given the most milk that day. Then the farmer simply walks in front of the cows and one by one they fall in line and head for home. My mother said that it seemed to her that the cow that had been awarded the flower wreath carried her head a little higher than the others. No whips or cattle prods are used on the cows in the Swiss Alps. They know well the voice of the farmer, and when he calls they turn toward him, knowing he will lead them home.

Jesus did not win his followers with threats or intimidation. It was not the fear of hell that bound them to his words. "Consider the lilies. Look for the lost lambs. Display mercy to those who don't deserve it. Feed the hungry. Clothe the poor." Those were the examples he gave his followers.

Jesus led them with cords of kindness.

Question

Pick one word that best and most honestly describes your leadership style.

- Intimidation
- Forcefulness
- Authority
- Kindness
- Other:_____

Question

Name someone in your past who led you with cords of kindness.

Question

Describe in detail what that cord was made of. What were the words, the thoughts, the deeds, that were braided into that cord?

Question

If you had to pick which is more powerful than the other, which would you choose: forcefulness or kindness? Why?

Question

Can a leader be powerful and kind at the same time? Why?

Power Connection:

Dear Lord, teach me to be kind. Let kindness become my overarching thought, my guiding light, and my compass. Let me understand that kindness is an eternal cord, leading others to You, and that it is woven one thread at a time.

Amen

I, _____, lead with cords of kindness.

He Honored His Appointment

Jesus said, "You did not choose me but *I* have chosen you and *appointed you* to do great works." —John 15:16. An appointment is a decision made by a person in authority to harness and utilize someone else's gifts for a higher purpose. It is not something necessarily sought or deserved or expected, and it can also be refused. Yet, a power-filled person honors this appointment.

Yet too many of us fail to keep even simple appointments. We show up late or not at all, or reschedule into oblivion. Whenever we do this, it almost always costs us business deals and/or strains relationships. The people who attain success are the ones who honor their appointments.

Saul was appointed King. But his impatience and jealousy caused him to "dishonor" that appointment. He eventually was killed, not by an enemy in battle, but because he fell on his own sword. When we do not honor God's appointment, we are in essence falling on our own swords. Our decision not to serve God and others goes against who we were created to be. Self-sabotage and slow suicide are sometimes the result of failing to honor our divine appointments.

To honor an appointment means to show up, unquestioningly, willing and ready to serve God. To honor an appointment means you do not argue with the Authority who appointed you—*or* downplay your gifts. To honor your appointment means to rise to the occasion and serve and give and trust. Husbands who do not nurture their wives, wives who do not cherish their husbands, children who do not respect their parents, employers who do not grow their employees, and employees who fail to honor their employers are all failing to honor their appointments. *"In all you do, be the master, and do not spoil the honor that is rightly yours."* —ECCLESIASTICUS 33:23 *The New Jerusalem Bible*

We must learn to honor ourselves.

When President Clinton appointed poet Maya Angelou to write his first inaugural poem, she did not recoil in fear or argue that perhaps others were better suited to the task. She took the assignment and created a riveting poem whose images haunt us still. She honored her appointment.

There is an air of mystery in Jesus' declaration, "You did not choose me—but I chose you." —John 15:16. I've long believed that the oft-quoted scripture, "No one comes to the Father except through me"—John 14:16, has as much to do with Jesus' appointment of us as followers as it does to his exclusionary access to the throne. He also said, "No one comes to me unless the Father draws (appoints) him."—John 14:16

We who know, and are known, by God have actually been appointed. We must honor that appointment as zealously as any Cabinet member or ambassador would.

> "And you, my child, will be called
> a prophet of the Most High;
> for you will go on before the Lord
> to prepare the way for him,
> to give his people the knowledge
> of salvation
> through the forgiveness of their sins.
> And the child grew and became
> strong in spirit, and he lived
> in the desert until he appeared
> publicly to Israel."
> —LUKE 1:76–80

Jesus honored his appointment.

Question

Do you honor your appointments—or do you show up late or cancel them?

Question

Do you believe God has appointed you? To do what?

Question

Do you honor your appointments in your relationships with others?

Question

Do you live up to the calling that those jobs demand?

Power Connection:

Dear Lord, You have appointed me to the task before me based on Your assessment of my talents and gifts. Help me accept this appointment with dignity, and recognize the honor and importance of this gift You have bestowed. Let me serve You exceedingly well.

Amen.

I, _____, honor my appointment.

He Was Willing to
Be a Beginner

One day it occurred to me that Jesus had a belly button. (Don't laugh—it came to me as a revelation.) This meant that at some point his umbilical cord to his mother had to have been cut, and he had to begin his time on earth just like the rest of us—drooling and cooing and gradually learning to make out familiar faces. Do you really think Jesus hit the ground running? Not so. He stumbled and crawled and bumped his head and had a spate of a two-year-old's bruises just like any active child. In his humility and profound desire to make a difference for others, he was willing to be a *beginner*. Jesus must have asked his mother, "How should I hold this lamb?" and his mother showed him. Jesus asked his father, "How should I cut this wood?" and his father showed him. He even had to have someone teach him how to read.

One of the most amazing concepts for me to grasp about Jesus was his willingness to be a beginner. He was willing to put down a scepter that could sway the stars and take up a crude wooden toy made by his carpenter father.

Jesus said, "Unless you become like a little child, you cannot even enter the kingdom of Heaven." —Luke 18:17. What is implied is that the kingdom of heaven is really for beginners. Those who think themselves full of knowledge about it won't even get in.

My friend and minister Wendy Craig Purcell once said that she would rather be a beginner in a field that held her interest than remain a master doing work she no longer cared about.

Considering the fact that most of us never utilize more than 10 percent of our total mental capacities in any endeavor, the opportunities we have to be beginners is limitless. Yet often as we grow up we quit asking questions. Once we decide that we must pretend to know, rather than ask, we have cut off any chance for advancing ourselves. One of the characteristics of power-filled people is that they have a ravenous curiosity about the world.

My friend Lisa is a brilliant former intensive-care nurse, who has become operations manager for a multimillion-dollar health-care consulting firm. One day she invited me to hear her play the piano. She'd been telling me about her lessons for several months and was extremely excited about them. When I came to visit her she made quite a production of getting her music out and unplugging the phone so we wouldn't be disturbed. She sat down to play, and I was surprised at what poured forth. It was a two-fingered children's song about a butterfly. Her finishing flourish included the use of two fingers on *each* hand hitting the keyboard simultaneously, which meant she ended not with a note, but with a *chord*. She looked up at me full of glee, "Isn't this fantastic!" she asked? "Yes!" I responded, "Bravo! Bravo!" Lisa is currently playing the piano at a child's level. Yet in her heart beats the spirit of all great masters, because she is willing to be a beginner.

Life is full of joyous and challenging skills to learn—so much so that even . . .

Jesus was willing to be a beginner.

Question

What new field would you like to master, even though it means starting as a beginner?

Question

Based on the number of questions you ask each day, how eager to learn are you?

Question

Name the people you admire who were willing to be beginners.

Dear Lord, help me have the curiosity of a little child. Help me be eager to learn something new each day, and never let me be content, thinking I know it all. Help me nurture and respect the beginner's spirit in others, remembering that even You had to learn before You were able to teach. Thank You for all teachers who so willingly share their knowledge with us, the many beginners.

Amen.

I, _____, am willing to be a beginner.

He Lived the Answer

The German poet Rainer Maria Rilke coined the expression, "Live the question." At several personal growth seminars I attended in California, those words became a favorite catchphrase in response to difficult and seemingly unresolvable issues. If you don't have the answer, "live the question." I enjoyed using the phrase myself for a while. But as I contemplated how that phrase applied to Jesus, it became clear to me that Jesus didn't live the question—he lived the *answer*.

What if each of us took a moment and looked at ourselves and realized, "In this difficult situation, I will live the answer"?

When Jesus encountered a sick or a discontented person he did not linger in philosophical discussions about how and why the person reached that state. Instead, he became the answer—and showed him or her how he or she could become part of the answer, too. "Your faith has made you well . . . Reach out your hand . . . Rise up and walk . . . Lazarus, come forth . . ." All of these were highly interactive exchanges about "becoming the answer."—Matthew 9:22; Mark 3:5, Luke 5:22, John 11:43

A statue of Jesus that had been damaged during the German bombing raids during World War II was fully intact except for its hands, which had been broken off during an attack. A passerby placed a sign at the base of the statue that read, "We are his hands."

As a baby boomer who was raised in an era of great promise and privilege, I am nonetheless unsettled to realize that, at nearly every level, my generation is now leading governments and institutions and schools and corporations. We are now the leaders we used to criticize. No longer can we luxuriate in the role of backseat drivers. Now *we* are making the decisions others complain about.

As a Christian I have often heard the question, "If God is so loving, why does he allow children to starve to death in Africa?" I believe part of the answer is "God doesn't allow it— we do."

It has been my observation that the people who have chosen to involve themselves in solving the earth's ills waste little time or energy on blaming God. They have decided to not live the question but to live the answer.

"My father goes on working and so do I."—John 5:17.

Jesus lived the answer.

Question

Name five people you know or know about who have chosen to live the answer, rather than dwell in the question.

Question

How are they doing so?

Question

In your particular situation how could you begin to live the answer?

Power Connection:

Dear Lord, today I am faced with many questions, some of which seem to have no answer. It is in these situations that I need to believe Your faith in me and rekindle mine in You. Help me not to stir in the question, but to live the answer.

Amen.

I, _____, live the answer.

He Was Event Oriented

Jesus conducted his first miracle at a wedding. He was a regular and willing guest at parties, funerals, picnics, seminars, and synagogue gatherings. When people assembled to hear him talk he wanted to make sure that they were fed, too. He knew full well that food could increase the absorption rate of certain spiritual principles. Jesus was *event* oriented.

As an advertising specialist I was trained early on to recognize the outreach value of "events." There is something about seeing a group of people with a similar range of interests that adds electricity to an atmosphere. Trade shows are becoming more and more popular as a means of presenting ideas and products because the average cost of an individual sales call far exceeds the cost of hosting an event.

Having worked one summer as an intern for a Congressman in Washington, D.C., I can tell you that the city is almost wall-to-wall, back-to-back events and parties and fund-raisers. It is at these gatherings that issues are discussed far more freely than in the prewritten and not so well-rehearsed scripts we see delivered on the Senate floor.

In his book *Managing to Have Fun*, Matt Weinstein suggests that we need to be more creative in seeing or making events out of little things. One secretary noted that her boss made it a big event when she finished a manuscript, presenting her with candy and flowers and little trumpets.

Each day, in fact, begins and ends with a grand event that we usually take for granted: Sunrise and sunset. God obviously loves to begin and close each day with a special, often spectacular flourish.

The seasons, also, are events. *Webster's* defines an event as "a happening of some importance." Aren't there many such happenings in your life? How many do you turn into events?

I often recommend that entrepreneurs who are launching a new business host an open house to show their friends and neighbors exactly what they do. Word of mouth is always the best advertising, and nowhere is it more frequently generated than at events or gatherings.

In the hilarious movie *To Wong Foo Thanks for Everything Julie Newmar*, three men notorious for turning everything into an event ponder the meager attempts of the town they have wound up in to build a sense of community. One of the more flamboyant characters says, "What this town needs is a party!" And voilà—the town is turned into a setting for a grand celebration. People dress up, the women get their hair done, the men clean their fingernails, the old band instruments are taken out, and banners abound. Soon, people who had over the years quit speaking to each other were suddenly dancing arm in arm. By deciding to celebrate *something* the whole town was transformed.

Since I believe that the Holy Spirit is not only a comforter but also a deep appreciator of events, I wholly recommend that each of us should look to hosting more celebrations.

Why do we spend so much time waiting for our ship to come in when instead we should be launching it? "Whenever *two* or more are gathered in my name, there I am in the midst of them."—Matthew 18:20

He was event oriented.

Question

What event could you sponsor that would bring attention to your cause or concern?

Question

What could you do to make it entertaining as well as educational?

Question

Who else might join forces with you in co-sponsoring such an event?

Power Connection:

Dear Lord, help me see the value of having people gather together—in celebration, in discussion, in delight. Fire my imagination with events. Cause me to create and trigger more exciting events in my community, my workplace, my home.

Amen.

I, _____, am event oriented.

He Created an Atmosphere

One of the most interesting and exciting experiences a new company or group can undertake is deciding the "atmosphere" they want to create. While many of us are not conscious of the atmosphere we are fostering, the truth is that our thoughts and energy go beyond our physical reach, and become an atmosphere that surrounds us.

Atmospheres are evident everywhere. Whether it is the cartoon character Pigpen walking around with a cloud of dirt above him or the scientific discussion about the depleting ozone layer in the earth's atmosphere, we are becoming more aware that there is an energy cloud around and above us that is a vital part of who we are.

To create an atmosphere requires that one consciously decide what kind of thoughts and behaviors will be encouraged and nurtured in it. We have all met people who maintain a "Woe is me" atmosphere. Likewise, others have laughter and play as their trademark "atmosphere."

Nearly any of us could walk into a company, a home, a restaurant, a building, and sense immediately what its atmosphere is. The atmosphere we are sensing is something that was created, either consciously or subconsciously, by the people in it.

Jesus created an atmosphere, or "corporate culture," all his own. By letting children run to him, rather than demanding that they stay quietly at their parents' sides, by speaking openly to women who formerly had been shunned, by asking questions and expressing emotions and attending nearly every party he was invited to Jesus was establishing an atmosphere of openness and love—an atmosphere that was very different from the one established by the religious leaders of that time.

Every deed we do has a ripple effect that either invites people to jump in, because the water's fine, or warns them in no uncertain terms to stay in their place—outsiders are not welcome.

When Dee Jones, my administrator, and I sat down to discuss what our corporate culture would be, we got more and more enthusiastic about designing an atmosphere in which we and others like us could thrive. We addressed such issues as office location (no big buildings), dress code (casual unless dress-up day is called for), structure (nonlinear and open), and attitudes (nonpontifical, nonjudgmental). We came up with our own slogans, such as, "We assign no blame and offer no excuses." We declared that everyone associated with us would be actively engaged in using their highest gifts—and that we would openly encourage others to do the same. We decided we would strive for divine excellence with all our talents and seek new and creative ways to carry out our mission—which is to produce products and programs that inspire divine connection. In essence, what we were doing was breathing a personality into an organization that at that moment consisted solely of written words on a page.

Families can and should consciously create together the atmosphere of their home. What kind of words and behaviors will be encouraged here? Which kind will not be allowed? What energy will people feel and notice when they walk into our home?

The Dutch artist Peter Paul Rubens created an atmosphere in his part of the world, even though technically he was only a painter. An intellectual gifted with visionary and diplomatic skills, as well as the ability to speak five languages, Rubens fostered an atmosphere for art in the Netherlands that became legendary. He imported ideas like others did jewels. He encouraged young artists to collaborate rather than compete with one another—actually producing masterpieces that were signed by *several* people. Rubens didn't just paint—he created an era, one that is now known as "The Age of Rubens."

When we begin to realize that our words, attitudes, and actions are literally producing an atmosphere, perhaps we will be more conscious of the ripple effect of our being. We aren't just creating words—we are creating atmospheres.

When Jesus looked at the dying child or at the woman caught in her past or even at the empty tombs that once housed the hearts of the scribes and the Pharisees, and called out "Live!" he was creating an atmosphere around him—one of openness and possibility and new beginnings.

Jesus created an atmosphere.

Question
Define "atmosphere."

Question
List the ways an atmosphere is created, encouraged, or sustained:
• in a home
• in a workplace
• in a religious institution
• in a relationship

Question
Like Rubens, are you painting your own individual pictures, or are you creating an "age"?

Describe the current atmosphere in:

- your workplace
- your home
- your family
- your primary relationship
- your place of worship

Power Connection:

Dear Lord, You have given us a beautiful, fragile atmosphere in which to thrive and grow. Help us to nurture and protect it and to be conscious of the atmosphere we create every day for those around us, through our words and attitudes.

Amen.

I, _____, create an atmosphere.

He Gave the Gift of His Presence

The one resource we all seem to be so desperately short of is time. Many of my friends literally gasp whenever I tell them what time it is, no matter what time it is. "What time is it?" they'll ask, matter of factly. "9 a.m." "Gasp!" Or . . . "3 p.m." "Gasp!" Whatever the time is, it feels like it is too late for them. They are constantly running "behind."

Perhaps because Jesus knew that he had all of eternity, he never seemed to "rush" anywhere. I can find no scripture that reads "And he rushed to . . ." Yet all of us seem to be in such a hurry these days. One cost of that perception (of being out of time) is that we forget to afford one another the simple yet magnificent, irreplaceable gift—the gift of our presence. Jesus understood the value of presence. It is in fact the only thing he ever really asked of his disciples. "Will you wait with me in the garden?" he asked as he faced the most difficult decision of his life.—Mark 14: 32–37. "Will you, too, leave me, Peter?" he asked when many people found his words too harsh for their taste.—John 6: 67–68. In his final prayer to God in John 17 he asks, "Father, may they be *with me* where I am."—John 17:24

I found it interesting when I surveyed Jesus' activities how great a priority he put on attending weddings, funerals, picnics, and dinner parties. The one common element in all of these is simply "being there." Sometimes our very presence is all that is needed. A poem I heard recently entreating fathers to spend more time with their children said "The toys and the presents will all fade away, but they'll never forget the gift of a day."

Several years ago when my mother was doing volunteer work with AIDS patients, she chose to work with a newborn baby girl named Nancy who was born with AIDS from a drug addicted mother. I tried to dissuade Mom from taking the case because I felt that getting attached to a child who was destined to die in a few years would be too heart wrenching for her. Mom persisted, however, and she went every day to be with Nancy, even if it was only for a few hours. She and several other people from her church group decided that Nancy was going to be the most loved, held, rocked, and sung to baby in the hospital ward. When Mom wasn't with Nancy she was knitting her booties, or making her blankets. The months went by. And then the most amazing thing happened. Nancy, for some reason which was a mystery at that time, began to get better. When they took her for her AIDS test again, she showed no signs of the disease. They retested her, a few months later, thinking it had been a mistake, and indeed, the virus was undetectable. Perhaps that determined group of volunteers had *helped* accelerate her healing simply through the gift of their presence.

A young woman named Ruth in the Old Testament changed history by her determination to give the gift of presence to her severely depressed mother-in-law, Naomi. "Whither you go, I will go. Your people will be my people, your God will be my God. Where you lie, I will lie" said Ruth, without hesitation, and she went with Naomi to Bethlehem. There she met and married Boaz, and gave birth to a son named Obed, who became the grandfather of King David. —Ruth 1–3

One of my friends is an army chaplain, and he emphasized to me one day the importance of "the ministry of presence." I never forgot his words, and began to look at situations with a new perspective. I soon got a chance to experience that, as one day when driving home from a road trip I came upon a horrible car accident in the deserts of Arizona, hundreds of miles from any town. I was one of the first persons on the scene. A van had flipped over, and five people were scattered on the highway. One woman was still trapped inside. Several other cars quickly stopped, and two of the people who came to render aid were a doctor and a Marine medic. As they quickly moved to check the ones who were most injured, and to free the woman still trapped inside,

I began to feel helpless. A voice inside me said "You did what you could. You called on your cellular phone for help. They have got everything under control. There's nothing more that you can do." Besides, I had friends expecting me. Many other cars who had slowed to help had obviously come to the same conclusion, and were driving off.

But then I remembered the words of my chaplain friend. "The ministry of presence." So I went to one of the victims who was just lying there alone. A teenaged boy, he had been determined by a doctor to have a broken arm, broken ankle, and broken ribs, but he would definitely survive. The doctor moved on to the more seriously injured. I sat down beside the boy and gave him some water. He was obviously in shock, but still managed to whisper his name, Mark. I told him my name was Laurie and asked him several questions, trying to carry on a conversation and keep him from going unconscious. The sun was hitting his face so I took a piece of cardboard and held it up to shade him. I just sat there beside him and prayed and talked and waved away the flies from the blood on his arms and legs while the medical people attended to his mother, who was in critical condition. Forty-five minutes later the ambulance and helicopter arrived from Phoenix. I stood and watched as the hospital team lifted Mark onto the stretcher. I walked beside him to the ambulance while they airlifted his mother out on the helicopter. He gave me a weak smile and a thumbs up sign as they closed the doors. I just stood there, shaking. I have never felt so helpless in my life. "Why hadn't

I learned CPR? Why couldn't I have had a more extensive first aid kit in my car? Why hadn't I gone to medical school?" These negative thoughts flooded over me and then I heard a very soft voice say, "In this situation you gave the one thing you did have, and that was your presence."

Recently a woman who was head of a church worship committee shared with me that their mission is "to accompany others into the presence of God." What could be more beautiful? Or more meaningful?

Sam Faraone is a police chaplain who volunteers to go to scenes where someone has to be informed of a relative's sudden death. He says that all he can do in those situations is offer prayers, and his presence. I asked him why a busy minister like him, with a family and a full congregation, would add to the stress in his life by going out at all hours to meet and share the shock and grief of strangers. He said simply, "I think it is something that Jesus would do."

In the book of Daniel three men who refuse to worship King Nebuchadnezzar are bound together and thrown into a furnace. "The king's command was so urgent and the furnace so hot that the flames of the fire killed the soldiers who threw the three men into the fire. Shadrach, Meshack, and Abednego fell together into the blazing inferno. Then King Nebuchadnezzar leaped to his feet in amazement and asked his advisers, "Weren't there three men that we tied up and threw into the fire?" They replied, "Certainly, O King." He said, "Look! I see *four* men walking around in the fire, unbound

and unharmed, and one of them looks like a son of the gods."
—Daniel 3: 13–25

"Lo, I am with you always."—Matthew 28:20

Jesus gave the gift of his presence.

Question

Are you always in a hurry?

Question

Who needs your presence, right now? In the days to come?

Question

Name a time from your past when someone gave you the gift of his or her presence. What did it mean to you?

Question

Name a time from your past when someone didn't give you the gift of his or her presence. How did that affect you?

Power Connection:

Dear Lord,

Help me understand that the one thing You want most from me is my presence. You created us to be *with You* in the

Garden of Eden, and Your son asked specifically if I could be *with him* in heaven. Help me realize that my presence is the one gift I can give, and that it is often the only gift that matters. Help me be more aware of Your presence in my life. Amen

I, _____, give the gift of my presence.

He Threw His Light Forward

"The Lord said to Moses, 'Tell Aaron that when he lights the seven lamps in the lampstand, he is to set them so that they will throw their light forward.' " —Numbers 8:1 (*The Living Bible*)

When I first read that verse it struck me as no coincidence that the light was supposed to shine forward, rather than in a random or haphazard fashion. Scholars say that every article in the tabernacle is symbolic of some aspect of our relationship with God and God's relationship with us. From what I have been able to discern of God's heart, he is most interested in having our light go *forward*.

Recently I overheard a political consultant say of a candidate who kept bemoaning all the changes happening in society, "Yes, this man is intent on leading us back to the 1950s." Perhaps we don't need to fear recession so much as regression—because the past is gone. It is over. What we have is the future, and we must go forward to meet it.

In Zechariah 8, "The Lord of Hosts says, 'Get on with the job and finish it! You have been listening long enough! For since you began laying the foundation of the Temple, the prophets have been telling you about the blessings that await you when it's finished. Before the work began there were no jobs, no wages, no security; if you left the city, there was no assurance you would ever return, for crime was rampant. But it is all so different now! For I am sowing peace and prosperity among you. Your crops will prosper; the grapevines will be weighted down with fruit; the ground will be fertile, with plenty of rain; all these blessings will be given to the people left in the land. 'May you be as poor as Judah,' the heathen used to say to those they cursed! But no longer! For now 'Judah' is a word of blessing, not a curse. 'May you be as prosperous and happy as Judah is,' they'll say. So don't be afraid or discouraged! Get on with rebuilding the Temple! If you do, I will certainly bless you." —Numbers 8: 1–14

There the Lord is exhorting the people to forget about their negative past and move forward into the new land of promise and prosperity. "Throw your light forward!" he is urging. "Do not look backward anymore."

When God was leading Lot and his wife out of the land of Sodom and Gomorrah, he warned them not to look back at the city. Lot's wife did and became a pillar of salt. Too often, when we look backward, we become pillars of salt, full of self-pity and regrets and self-loathing and blame. "None of that!"

God seems to be saying. "Throw your candlelight forward." I repeat this thought to myself often, especially when I become immobilized by memories of things I wish I'd done differently.

The more we ponder mistakes we've made, the more we are afraid to move, fearing that we will only carry our mistakes into the future. *Throw your light forward,* God's word reminds us. Write that next book. Make that next phone call. Don't worry about the past. Keep moving forward.

> *My love lifts up his voice,*
> *he says to me,*
> *"Come then, my beloved,*
> *my lovely one, come.*
> *For see, winter is past,*
> *the rains are over and gone.*
> *Flowers are appearing on the earth*
> *The season of glad songs*
> *has come."*
> SONG OF SOLOMON 2:10–12
> (NEW JERUSALEM BIBLE)

Jesus threw his light forward.

Question

Where in your life are you using your light to look backward?

Question

How does the message "throw your light forward" relate to your life today?

Question

What do you claim is preventing you from going forward?

Question

What would God's opinion of your thinking on that be?

Power Connection:

Dear Lord, I cannot change the past. I can only move forward. Help me grasp the light that You have given me, and continue to give me, and help me use that to light my future steps and actions. Help me be a beacon, not a pillar of salt. Let me set the candlesticks in the temple—so that my light goes forward. Help me see that the rain is over and gone.

Amen.

I, _____, throw my light forward.

Gift Offer

For more information, to get on our mailing list, or to order any of the following please contact:

The Jesus, CEO Foundation
813 Summersong Court
Encinitas, CA 92024
Phone: 760-753-7251
Fax: 760-634-2707
e-mail www.jnsgroup@aol.com
website www.lauriebethjones.com

If you would like to receive a free bookmark from *Jesus in Blue Jeans*, please send us a stamped, self-addressed #10 (11 inch long) envelope, and we will also include you on our mailing list.

If you have had a dramatic self-prophecy or positive prophecy from others about you come true, please also mail, fax, or e-mail that to us, and we will possibly include that in one of our upcoming books. Deadline for story submissions is May 1998.

We also have the following products and services available:

Keynote speaking
Full- or half-day on-site leadership training programs

Study guides for *Jesus, CEO* and *The Path*
Facilitator's training in *Jesus, CEO* and *The Path*
On-line college courses on *Jesus, CEO* and *The Path*
Personal telephone consultations with Laurie
A master's / mentor program for individuals
Songtape and coloring book for children
A newsletter

Acknowledgments

My goal is to pour more beauty and inspiration into the world, and this takes a team, as well as a dream. Many thanks therefore are owed to Rick Kot, my editor, and Michael Liss, his assistant, and to Bob Miller, my publisher at Hyperion, who showed so much enthusiasm for the content. I am grateful for my agent, Julie Castiglia, and for Dee Jones, my administrator, who keeps me sane. I most especially want to thank you, the readers, whose stories and smiles and prayers and tears have inspired me to keep writing, and to the bookstore sales staff and distributors whose efforts ensure that books are available when people need and want them.

I would like to thank the following people who have been recent and ongoing champions of *Jesus, CEO* and *The Path*: Judith Addington of Gazelle Productions, Franklin Beach of Groom Industries, Pat Bessey of Unity Church of Overland Park, Betty Ann Bird of Quest Leadership, Judy

Budd of St. Joseph Medical Center, Catherine Calhoun of Calhoun & Associates, Michael Cardone Jr. of Cardone Industries, Don Collins and Charles Waldo of Anderson University, Dr. Andrew Colyer of Parkland Pain & Rehab Clinic, Wendy Craig-Purcell of the Church of Today, Lisa Dahlberg of the New Zealand Productivity and Quality Centre, Reverend Howard Eddington of the First Presbyterian Church of Orlando, Sandra Foyil of Our Lady of Lourdes Medical Center, Dr. Arlan Fuhr of Activator Methods, Bill and Gloria Gaither of the Gaither Music Company, Pastor Tim Garrison of the Camarillo Seventh Day Adventist Church, Dr. Jerry Haddock of the Association of Christian Schools International, Billy Bob Harris of RCS Investments, Sally Hazard of Menlo Park Presbyterian Church, Karen Hruby of Michigan State University College of Osteopathic Medicine, Reverend Lawrence Kent of the First Presbyterian Church of Flint, Brad Lindemann of Ambassador Consulting, George Longshore of Longshore and Simmons, Reverend Mother M. de Chantal St. Julien of the Sisters of the Holy Family, Ed McLaughlin of Holy Redeemer Health System, Nancy McNamee of Mississippi Madness, Ray Napolitano, Odile Nicolette of The Inside Edge, Beth O'Dower of San Diego Women's Network/NAFE, Deborah Shaw of Umbrellas Plus, Steven Shull of Performance Coaching, Tammy Czyzewski, MS, RN of Kettering Medical Center, Gerald Summers of A.G. Edwards, Inc., Carol Suter of the Mennonite Economic Development Association, Judy Taylor of the Leading Edge, Joe Tye of Never Fear, Never Quit, Rose Marie Greco of Core States Financial, Millard Fuller of Habitat for Humanity, Mark Virkler of Christian Leadership University, Kingsley Fletcher of Fletcher Group International, Bob and Cindy DiBaudo, Nancy Haney, Attorney at Law, Jeff Cohen, Attorny at Law, Bonnie Worthley, and Pastor Bill Watson of Brookridge Community Church.

Jonna Morfessis of the Greater Phoenix Economic Development Council, Tino Ballesteros and Robert Schuller of the Crystal Cathedral, Richard Stenbakken of Seventh-Day Adventist Ministries, Annette Swanberg and Lucinda Dyer of Swanberg & Dyer.

Index

300